# JESSICA TANDY

**Recent Titles in**
**Bio-Bibliographies in the Performing Arts**

Ann Sothern: A Bio-Bibliography
*Margie Schultz*

Alice Faye: A Bio-Bibliography
*Barry Rivadue*

Orson Welles: A Bio-Bibliography
*Bret Wood*

Jennifer Jones: A Bio-Bibliography
*Jeffrey L. Carrier*

Cary Grant: A Bio-Bibliography
*Beverley Bare Buehrer*

Maureen O'Sullivan: A Bio-Bibliography
*Connie J. Billips*

Ava Gardner: A Bio-Bibliography
*Karin J. Fowler*

Jean Arthur: A Bio-Bibliography
*Arthur Pierce and Douglas Swarthout*

Donna Reed: A Bio-Bibliography
*Brenda Scott Royce*

Gordon MacRae: A Bio-Bibliography
*Bruce R. Leiby*

Irene Dunne: A Bio-Bibliography
*Margie Schultz*

Mary Martin: A Bio-Bibliography
*Barry Rivadue*

# JESSICA TANDY

## A Bio-Bibliography

MILLY S. BARRANGER

Bio-Bibliographies in the Performing Arts,
Number 22

**GREENWOOD PRESS**
New York • Westport, Connecticut • London

**Library of Congress Cataloging-in-Publication Data**

Barranger, Milly S.
Jessica Tandy : a bio-bibliography / Milly S. Barranger.
p. cm.—(Bio-bibliographies in the performing arts, ISSN 0892-5550 ; no. 22)
Includes bibliographical references and index.
ISBN 0-313-27716-8 (alk. paper)
1. Tandy, Jessica. 2. Tandy, Jessica—Bibliography. 3. Actors—United States—Biography. I. Title. II. Series.
PN2287.T16B37 1991
792'.028'092—dc20
[B] 91-25094

British Library Cataloguing in Publication Data is available.



Library of Congress Catalog Card Number: 91-25094
ISBN: 0-313-27716-8
ISSN: 0892-5550

First published in 1991

Greenwood Press, 88 Post Road West, Westport, CT 06881
An imprint of Greenwood Publishing Group, Inc.

Printed in the United States of America

The paper used in this book complies with the Permanent Paper Standard issued by the National Information Standards Organization (Z39.48-1984).

10 9 8 7 6 5 4 3 2 1

# Contents


| | |
|---|---|
| Preface | vii |
| Biography | 1 |
| Chronology | 13 |
| Stage Appearances | 29 |
| Filmography | 65 |
| Television Appearances | 109 |
| Discography | 113 |
| Awards and Nominations | 117 |
| Bibliography | 121 |
| Subject Index | 139 |

# Preface

This book serves as a comprehensive reference to the distinguished career of actress Jessica Tandy. Included here are all of the major details of her life and career--in theatre, film, television, recordings, and interviews.

The book begins with a biography and chronology setting forth the major events of her life in theatre and film. Tandy was born, educated and trained for the stage in London. She began her professional stage career with a British repertory company and in commercial productions on London's West End. She first came to the United States in productions transferred to Broadway from the West End. During the war years she took up permanent residence in the United States, established a second family, became a Hollywood bit player, and won the part of Blanche DuBois in a new play by Tennessee Williams called A Streetcar Named Desire.

Two years on Broadway as the celebrated Blanche DuBois established Tandy's reputation as a renowned international actress. Since that time she, and her husband Hume Cronyn, have sustained distinguished careers in American theatre and film for fifty years. They have been called a "new generation" Alfred Lunt and Lynn Fontanne to explain their position in the American theatre as a stage couple. They have appeared frequently together in film and on stage, beginning with The Fourposter in 1951.

Not until 1989 did Tandy emerge as more than a minor player in British and American films. Despite her Broadway triumph in A Streetcar Named Desire, she lost the film role of Blanche DuBois to another British actress--Vivien Leigh. Thirty-eight years later, Tandy won the major film role of her career and the elusive Oscar award as Daisy Werthan in Driving Miss Daisy.

Today, Jessica Tandy's name is synonymous with such stage roles as Blanche DuBois, Louise Harrington, Fonsia Dorsey, and Annie Nations, and with the film role of Miss Daisy Werthan. Memorable for the creation of roles in plays by Tennessee Williams, Edward Albee, and Samuel Beckett, Tandy is best remembered for her appearance in A

Streetcar Named Desire that serves as a hallmark in a stage and film career spanning fifty years.

## Format

This book begins with chapters entitled Biography and Chronology. The next four chapters detail Tandy's major career achievements, including stage appearances, filmography, television appearances, and discography. The individual entries in each of these four sections correspond to a particular career achievement and are numbered consecutively for convenient use in the subject index. Career events in each section are listed chronologically, then numbered consecutively. Stage appearances begin with **S01**, the filmography entries with **F01**, television appearances with **T01**, and the discography entries with **D01**. All dates in the filmography refer to the date of a film's release. The discography includes the title of the recording, the releasing company, the year of the release in parentheses, and finally the manufacturer order number.

A fifth chapter, entitled "Awards and Nominations," includes a list of various theatre, film and television awards that Tandy has either been nominated for or has won. These awards include Tonys, Drama Desk Awards, Obies, an Oscar and an Emmy, along with other awards and honorary degrees.

Following the listings of her work on stage, in film, television and on recordings, a bibliography includes more than 100 reference sources on Tandy's career, including books, magazine and newspaper feature articles and interviews. The book entries are numbered consecutively from **B01** and the newspaper/magazine articles from **R01**.

The final section, a subject index, includes page numbers and/or section entry numbers (for example **F01**) for easy reference. In some cases, page numbers seemed the most efficient way for the reader to locate a topic or an individual. In other cases, the section entry number seemed more helpful.

The overview of Jessica Tandy's career provided in this bio-bibliography describes the life of a professional actress who worked consistently in the media--stage, film, and television. Her distinguished reputation rested largely on her stage roles until the release of Driving Miss Daisy in 1989. Heretofore, Jessica Tandy had been a household name among theatregoers but today with the release of this major film and her Oscar award for Best Actress, she has emerged as a popular media figure.

## Acknowledgments

In the preparation of this book I am indebted to Jessica Tandy for her kind assistance, Tandy Cronyn for her friendship, David Hammond for his generous sharing of biographical materials gathered for another project, and Larry Warner for his resources on discography.

# Biography

Jessica Tandy, whose international stage career spans six decades, still reigns as the Tennessee Williams heroine against which every actress must be judged in the playing of A Streetcar Named Desire. In 1947, following a distinguished career in England and the United States, Tandy walked on the stage of Broadway's Ethel Barrymore Theatre as Blanche DuBois and spoke Williams' famous lines:

> They told me to take a street-car named Desire, and then transfer to one called Cemeteries and ride six blocks and get off at--Elysian Fields!

Brooks Atkinson, critic for The New York Times, called her performance as Williams' rueful heroine the "perfect marriage of acting and playwriting." Jessica Tandy's name has since become legendary, largely associated with classical stage roles and with premier works by Tennessee Williams, Edward Albee, and Samuel Beckett.

Born June 7, 1909 in Upper Clapton, London, Jessie Alice Tandy was the youngest of three children of Harry Tandy, a commercial traveler for a rope-manufacturing firm, and Jessie Helen (Horspool) Tandy, headmistress of a school for mentally-retarded children. Her father died of cancer when she was twelve. To support the family her mother subsequently took clerical jobs and taught evening classes for adults. They lived in a five-room brick house in the northeast London district of Hackney while Mrs. Tandy struggled to provide for her children's education and Jessie attended Dame Alice Owen's Girls' School. Mrs. Tandy instilled in her children an interest in literature, art, and theatre. Home theatricals and visits to museums were popular (and affordable) family pastimes, and money was carefully saved for trips to plays and pantomimes.

Mrs. Tandy's concern for the children's education resulted in the two Tandy boys, Arthur Harry ("Michael") and Edward James ("Tully"), winning scholarships to Oxford University. Childhood bouts with tuberculosis forced

Jessie to miss school frequently, making higher education and a teaching career like her mother's seem unrealistic goals for her. An alternative possibility soon emerged, for at the age of thirteen Jessie began to accompany her mother to her evening classes to avoid being left alone at home. She enrolled in adult courses in Shakespeare, poetry, dancing, and calisthenics during the hours her mother was teaching. She continued the Shakespeare classes for two years and, with her mother's encouragement, began working on Saturdays with a private drama coach. "My mother...endorsed the stage as a dignified way for me out of our bleak existence," Tandy said in an interview. "It sounds terribly snobbish, but she raised us to be intellectually above our neighbors. She read to us, took us to plays, the pantomime, and museums." (The New York Times Magazine 12/26/82)

At age fifteen she enrolled as a full-time student at London's Ben Greet Academy of Acting, the most prestigious training-ground for actors of its day. There, instructor Lillian E. Simpson became a powerful influence in guiding Tandy's emerging talent.

Three years later Tandy completed her studies and immediately began professional work, making her stage debut at age eighteen on November 22, 1927 in The Manderson Girls at Playroom Six in the Soho district of London. The next season, she joined the Birmingham Repertory Company, one of England's new regional companies, and appeared in Alice Sit-by-the-Fire and The Comedy of Good and Evil before touring for six months with the company in Yellow Sands. She made her London West End debut on February 21, 1929 as Lena Jackson in The Rumour.

She was now working steadily as a professional actress and playing a wide variety of roles both in England and the United States. On the West End, she was seen as The Typist in The Theatre of Life, Maggie in Water, and The Betrothed in The Unknown Warrior with Maurice Evans. She first appeared in New York on Broadway at the Longacre Theatre on March 18, 1930 as Toni Rakonitz in The Matriarch opposite Constance Collier in the title role. At the insistence of producer Lee Shubert, she changed her stage name to "Jessica" and appeared for the first time as Jessica Tandy. Brooks Atkinson praised the newcomer for playing with "fresh sincerity." The following summer she played her first Shakespearean role, appearing as Olivia in Twelfth Night with the Oxford University Dramatic Society. She then returned briefly to Broadway as Cynthia Perry in The Last Enemy. In the next two years she appeared in eight London productions, notable among them being Autumn Crocus, in which she enjoyed her first extended West End run and met husband-to-be Jack Hawkins who played opposite her.

In 1931, Tandy was cast in her first film role in the British production of The Indiscretions of Eve (released the next year). In the spring of 1932 she joined the Cambridge Festival Theatre for a repertory season of classic and modern plays. She appeared in Troilus and Cressida, See Naples and Die, The Witch, Rose Without a

Thorn, The Inspector General, and The Servant of Two Masters before returning to the West End as Carlotta in Mutual Benefit. The performance that firmly established her reputation as a gifted young actress was Manuela in Children in Uniform which opened at the Duchess Theatre on October 7, 1932. That same year she was married to actor Jack Hawkins and their daughter Susan Phyllida was born in 1934.

The next eight years established a pattern in what was emerging as a distinguished career on the British stage. At age twenty-four, Tandy balanced performances in over a dozen popular West End plays with an increasing number of appearances in classical roles. In 1933, she followed appearances in Lady Audley's Secret and Midsummer Fires on the West End with a performance as Titania in A Midsummer Night's Dream at the Open Air Theatre in Regent's Park, London. Subsequent Shakespearean roles included Viola in Twelfth Night and Anne Page in The Merry Wives of Windsor in 1934 at the Hippodrome in Manchester, England. In November of that year she was an acclaimed Ophelia to John Gielgud's Hamlet at the New Theatre in the West End which ran for 155 performances. Other West End performances followed.

Then in February 1937, she joined the Old Vic Company in London playing both Viola and Sebastian in Twelfth Night to Laurence Olivier's Sir Toby Belch. She called the production a romp and said her greatest difficulty was keeping a straight face when Olivier poked Sebastian in the chest to see what kind of man he was. (Cottrell 123) Then in April she played Katharine to Olivier's Henry V. Both productions were staged by Tyrone Guthrie who would also become an influence in Tandy's American stage career.

During the next two years Tandy appeared in the film Murder in the Family with Roddy McDowall. She next appeared on Broadway as Kay in J. B. Priestley's Time and the Conways with Sybil Thorndike. Returning to England, she played in Glorious Morning in the West End and returned again to Broadway in Paul Vincent Carroll's The White Steed. Criss-crossing the Atlantic Ocean, she played another Viola in Twelfth Night in Regent's Park Open Air Theatre, after which she joined a repertory company tour of Canada. She played again in New York in January of 1940 in the short-lived Geneva by George Bernard Shaw and then returned in the spring to the Old Vic, appearing as Cordelia to John Gielgud's King Lear under the direction of Harley Granville-Barker and as Miranda to Gielgud's Prospero in The Tempest.

Again in June-July of 1940 Tandy crossed the Atlantic Ocean, accompanied by her six year-old daughter, to appear on Broadway in A. J. Cronin's Jupiter Laughs. Now estranged from husband Jack Hawkins who was serving in the wartime British army, Tandy decided to take up permanent residence in the United States and attempt to establish a full-time career in New York and Hollywood. Both her career and her personal life took unexpected turns.

After several minor roles on Broadway, Tandy was struggling to earn a living. "That was a tough time," she admitted to Chris Chase in an interview years later. "I got to that stage where I felt I'd made it up," she said, "I never could act, I didn't act well. I'd lost it." (The New York Times 3/24/74) Her prospects brightened when she moved to Hollywood and was given a five-year contract with Metro-Goldwyn-Mayer and later with Twentieth Century-Fox. However, she was never viewed as a leading film actress and even as late as 1950 lost the film role of Blanche DuBois to another British actress--Vivien Leigh.

In the early 1940s, she met Canadian-born actor Hume Cronyn who became her second husband after both had settled in Hollywood. They were married on September 27, 1942 and their two children were born in California. Christopher Hume Cronyn was born on July 22, 1943 and Tandy Cronyn on November 26, 1945. In 1945 the Cronyns also legally adopted Susan Hawkins. Christopher has become a film production manager, Tandy an actress, and Susan, for a brief time a teacher, is married to John Tettemer. The Tettemers have four children. Jessica Tandy became a naturalized American citizen in 1952.

In their several years on the West coast, Tandy found few film opportunities while Cronyn worked with some frequency as a character actor and occasional screenwriter. At the time she wryly observed: "Hume is working. I am just sitting here perfecting cooking recipes--and getting worse and worse at it all the time." (The Playmakers 96)

Under contract to MGM, Tandy appeared with her husband and Spencer Tracy in The Seventh Cross and played supporting roles in The Valley of Decision and The Green Years. For Twentieth Century-Fox she played in Dragonwyck and Forever Amber and some years later in The Desert Fox with James Mason as Field Marshal Erwin Rommel. Her first leading role in film finally came with A Woman's Vengeance, released by Universal-International in 1947.

After five years away from the theatre and relative inactivity in a number of minor film roles, Tandy wanted very much to revive her stage career. "There came a point when I felt," she said, "that I just had to act in a play again." (Showcase) That she would be cast in the greatest role of a lifetime is one of the American theatre's legendary stories.

In the summer of 1947 a national search was underway by producer, director, and playwright to cast the leading roles in a new play by Tennessee Williams called A Streetcar Named Desire. All agreed that Bette Davis was the "ideal" choice but she was unavailable. Actresses Margaret Sullavan, Pamela Brown, and Mary Martin were discussed as possible choices but producer Irene M. Selznick remarked that in the absence of Bette Davis there was no "hands-down choice for Blanche." (A Private View 300)

At the time, Hume Cronyn held under option several one-act plays by Tennessee Williams. In January 1946, he directed his wife in a Los Angeles Actor's Laboratory

Theatre production of Portrait of a Madonna, the story of the tormented Miss Lucretia Collins who lives in a world of romantic illusions and finally ends in a mental institution. Tandy's performance at the Las Palmas Theatre received widespread acclaim and standing ovations from Hollywood audiences. On a trip earlier to the East coast Cronyn had gone to see Audrey Wood, Tennessee Williams' agent, to thank her for giving permission for several performances of Portrait of a Madonna. While he was in her office, Wood mentioned that she had a new script by Williams and permitted Cronyn to read the play. When he returned the script to her, Wood asked him, "Who do you think could play Blanche?" Without a moment's hesitation Cronyn replied, "Jessica Tandy." Audrey Wood considered his response for a moment and then replied, "You may be right." (The New York Times 11/28/48)

Cronyn had hoped that Tennessee Williams would come to Los Angeles to see Portrait of a Madonna that January, but it took until July (and the urgency of a scheduled opening for Streetcar before year's end) for producer Irene M. Selznick and director Elia Kazan to persuade the reluctant playwright to travel to Hollywood. By coincidence, Cronyn revived Portrait of a Madonna for two weeks during the summer. The Streetcar associates attended a performance and the matter of who would play Blanche DuBois on Broadway was settled. In their separate writings years later, all three unanimously agreed that the moment they witnessed Tandy's performance as Miss Lucretia Collins, she had won the role of Blanche DuBois. However, it was not quite that simple. Following the performance of Portrait of a Madonna, Kazan held several sessions with Tandy reading the script. A subsequent session with Irene Selznick resulted in a run-of-the-play contract for Tandy.

A Streetcar Named Desire opened at the Ethel Barrymore Theatre on December 3, 1947 with its now legendary cast: Jessica Tandy as Blanche DuBois, Marlon Brando as Stanley Kowalski, Karl Malden as Mitch, and Kim Hunter as Stella. Tandy's performance for two years on Broadway not only resurrected her stage career but established her as a preeminent actress of the American theatre. Brooks Atkinson, writing two reviews for The New York Times, described Tandy's performance in one of the longest and most exacting parts in the contemporary theatre. His praise for her performance was unqualified.

> ...She plays it with an insight as vibrant and pitiless as Mr. Williams' writing, for she catches on the wing the terror, the bogus refinement, the intellectual alertness and the madness that can hardly be distinguished from logic and fastidiousness. Miss Tandy acts a magnificent part magnificently. (The New York Times 12/14/47)

Other reviewers spoke of her performance as "brilliant" and

"memorable" and extolled her talent, intelligence, and discipline.

The play was awarded the Pulitzer Prize and the New York Drama Critics Circle Award, and Tandy received her first Antoinette Perry ("Tony") Award for Best Actress along with the Twelfth Night Club Award. This was not to be the end of the Streetcar story. In 1949 while Streetcar was still playing on Broadway, Laurence Olivier optioned the play for his wife, Vivien Leigh. The London production, directed by Olivier, opened in November of 1949 at the Aldwych Theatre on the West End to generally unfavorable reviews. The British public was largely shocked that Lady Olivier would perform in such a dissolute play ("a public indecency"), but all agreed that Vivien Leigh's performance was brilliant. Harold Hobson, reviewer for The Sunday Times, wrote:

> ...I do not know which to admire the more, the power, the emotion, of this performance, or the courage that enables Miss Leigh to go on giving it, with undimmed lustre, amidst these foolish suggestions that her play is a public indecency. (The Sunday Times, London 11/13/49)

When it was learned that the subsequent film of A Streetcar Named Desire was being cast in Hollywood, Vivien Leigh, as she had done for the role of Scarlett O'Hara two decades earlier, campaigned for and won the coveted film role of Blanche DuBois. Though Tandy's Broadway colleagues--Marlon Brando, Kim Hunter, and Karl Malden--performed in the screen version under the play's original director, Elia Kazan, Tandy was not to recreate her stage role on film. Conjecture has it that Tandy was not considered "box office" in films and without question Vivien Leigh's Scarlett O'Hara in Gone With the Wind was emblazoned on the memory of filmgoers worldwide.

Mindful of her stage success in A Streetcar Named Desire, Tandy concentrated now on her stage career. "Streetcar," she told Samuel G. Freedman in an interview, "gave me back the challenge, and the challenge has never left me." (The New York Times 11/27/83) In 1950, she played another neurotic character searching for happiness in the title role of Samson Raphaelson's Hilda Crane on Broadway that was directed by Hume Cronyn. She and Cronyn now wanted to work together on stage. Rather than waiting for an appropriate vehicle to be presented to them, Hume Cronyn generated their own production and they appeared jointly in Jan de Hartog's popular two-character play The Fourposter in 1951. The Fourposter ran for 632 performances and established the Cronyns firmly in the public mind as an acting duo. Their subtle teamwork and complementary acting styles in this series of vignettes recounting thirty-five years in the lives of a married couple earned high praise. Tandy and Cronyn shared a

Commoedia Matinee Club Bronze Medallion for their performances. Following the New York run at the Ethel Barrymore Theatre, the Cronyns toured the play extensively across the United States.

Through the years Tandy and Cronyn have appeared separately as well as together as a popular theatrical team rivaled only in American stage history by the famous Lunts--Alfred Lunt and Lynn Fontanne. Their daughter, Tandy Cronyn, credits her father's entrepreneurial efforts with nurturing their joint talents in general and her mother's artistic life in particular during Tandy's lean years in film and theatre.

Beginning with The Fourposter, the Cronyns appeared together in such two-character plays as Happy Days, The Gin Game, and The Petition. In the 1950s, they contributed to the early stages of several major theatrical movements: the developing Off-Broadway theatre and the emerging regional theatre. In 1953, Tandy and Cronyn joined the new Phoenix Theatre for its opening production Off-Broadway, a revival of Sidney Howard's Madam, Will You Walk, originally produced in 1936 with George M. Cohan. In a similar spirit of support for emerging theatres as alternatives to Broadway they repeated their performances in The Fourposter at reduced salaries for the New York City Center's popularly-priced revival series in 1955. Critics were once again extravagant in their praise of the Cronyns' performances. In 1961, Tandy joined the newly-formed American Shakespeare Festival in Stratford, Connecticut, to play Lady Macbeth and Cassandra (Troilus and Cressida) in repertory.

In 1963, the couple joined Tyrone Guthrie's Minnesota Theatre Company in Minneapolis for its inaugural season. This proved a highly significant and far-reaching contribution to the fledgling regional theatre movement. Tandy and Cronyn were the first major American stars to join a regional theatre on a full-time basis and Tyrone Guthrie's pioneering effort to establish an American regional theatre gained impetus and legitimacy through their presence during that first season. Tandy appeared as Gertrude in Hamlet, Olga in The Three Sisters, and as Linda Loman in Death of a Salesman. They returned again to the Guthrie Theater in 1965 where Tandy appeared as Madame Ranevskaya in The Cherry Orchard, Lady Wishfort in The Way of the World, and as a "peasant" in The Caucasian Chalk Circle. The Cronyns appeared again in 1982 at the Guthrie Theater where, with Tandy in the role of Annie Nations, they performed in a pre-Broadway try-out of Foxfire.

As further proof of their commitment to the regional theatre movement and their opportunity to perform again in a classical repertoire, the couple joined the Center Theatre Group at the Mark Taper Forum in Los Angeles for a 1968 version of Moliere's The Miser, based on a production in which Cronyn had first appeared at the Guthrie Theater in Minneapolis. Tandy played Frosine to Cronyn's Harpagon. The following summer Tandy joined the Shaw Festival at Niagara-on-the-Lake in Canada, playing Hesione Hushabye in

Heartbreak House. Tandy also worked with New York City's struggling Repertory Theatre of Lincoln Center in 1970 to play Marguerite Gautier in a revival of Tennessee Williams' Camino Real and returned again with Cronyn in 1972 for a Samuel Beckett Festival directed by Alan Schneider where they appeared together in Happy Days and Tandy appeared separately as Beckett's single presence in Not I. She received the Drama Desk Award for her performances in both plays by Samuel Beckett and a Village Voice Off-Broadway ("Obie") Award for Not I. One reviewer spoke of her "torrential voice" in Not I as like a "waterfall of insensate feeling." (The New York Times 11/23/72)

Robin Phillips, then artistic director of Ontario's Stratford Shakespeare Festival Theatre, persuaded the Cronyns to join the company for the 1976 season. Tandy appeared as Hippolyta/Titania to Cronyn's Bottom in A Midsummer Night's Dream, as Lady Wishfort in The Way of the World, and in the premiere of Larry Fineberg's Eve. She attracted major critical attention to Robin Phillips' subsequent attempt to produce plays in repertory at the Theatre London in Ontario where she gave, by all accounts, a shattering performance as Mary Tyrone in Eugene O'Neill's Long Day's Journey into Night, a role she later repeated at the Stratford Shakespeare Festival.

For almost two decades the Cronyns alternated regional theatre performances with Broadway productions. Thus, began Tandy's renewed association after many years with directors Tyrone Guthrie and John Gielgud. Moreover, she was to discover in Alan Schneider a director of extraordinary ability and insight, especially in regard to the new works by Samuel Beckett and Edward Albee.

On the Broadway stage in the 1950s, the Cronyns followed their joint success in The Fourposter with The Honeys in 1955, The Man in the Dog Suit in 1958, and the 1959 Triple Play (a bill of one-acts in which Tandy repeated her performance as Miss Lucretia Collins in Portrait of a Madonna along with roles in two short plays by Sean O'Casey). In December of 1959, Tandy appeared at the Music Box Theatre under John Gielgud's direction in Peter Shaffer's Five Finger Exercise, winning critical praise and the Delia Austrian Medal of the New York Drama League for her performance as Louise Harrington, a role in which she subsequently toured. (She had not worked with Gielgud since their successful Miranda/Prospero casting in The Tempest for the Old Vic in the thirties.) As the wealthy, snobbish Louise Harrington whose strained relations with her uncultured husband and independent son are brought to a deadly climax by her daughter's tutor, Tandy riveted audiences for 337 performances. Brooks Atkinson called her "brilliant" and others considered this her finest work since Streetcar. Tandy toured in the play for seven months. This was followed by two Broadway productions with Cronyn, including Big Fish, Little Fish, in which she joined him in a supporting role when the 1962 New York production moved to the Duke of York's Theatre in London. The second was Friedrich Duerrenmatt's critically esteemed but financially unsuccessful The Physicists at the Martin Beck Theatre in 1964. On September 12, 1966, the couple returned to the Martin Beck Theatre in Edward Albee's A Delicate Balance as Agnes and Tobias, a complacent suburban couple forced to reevaluate their marriage and their relationships with their best friends. The much-praised production, directed by Alan Schneider, won a Pulitzer Prize for its author and a Leland Powers Honorary Award for Tandy. "Jessie's understanding of her character was almost instinctive," Schneider wrote in his autobiography, "her voice, as well as every move she made was like music." (Entrances 375-76) Both Tandy and Cronyn remained with the production for its national tour.

Tandy joined the Broadway cast of British playwright David Storey's Home in January 1971 as a replacement for Dandy Nichols where she was reunited with friends John Gielgud and Ralph Richardson in a production imported from London's Royal Court Theatre. The dour Marjorie was very different from Tandy's other roles. She explained: "If you go on doing what you know you can do, and what you've done before, it would be dull." (The New York Times 3/24/74) Later that same season, she appeared under Gielgud's direction in another Albee premiere, All Over, which despite Tandy's bravura performance and excellent reviews for cast and director closed after forty-two performances at the Morosco Theatre.

The Cronyns next toured together in Promenade All by David E. Robison and then opened at the Ethel Barrymore Theatre in a popular production of Noel Coward in Two Keys, two one-act plays (Come into the Garden Maude and A Song at Twilight) in which both played pairs of beautifully contrasted roles as different occupants of the same hotel suite. In the curtain-raiser Tandy was impeccable as the blue-haired social-climber Anna-Mary Conklin and as the sympathetic but abused Hilde Latymer in A Song at Twilight. In an interview with Mel Gussow on their forty years in the theatre, the Cronyns talked about "adaptability" as the key to survival in the theatre. Commenting on their twin careers, Tandy said, "Our private life has not been wrenched apart, although it has been stretched a bit." (The New York Times 3/1/74) Their Broadway performances in Two Keys were followed once more by a successful national tour.

In 1977, the regional theatre movement reached again into the Cronyns' lives. Hume Cronyn was shown a new script of D. L. Coburn's The Gin Game, a two-character play originally produced by the Actors Theatre of Louisville in Kentucky. This was the author's first produced work, but Cronyn did not hesitate to option the script for future production. With Mike Nichols directing, The Gin Game opened at the John Golden Theatre on October 6, 1977, with Tandy and Cronyn as two lonely inmates of a nursing home. This production was another highpoint in both their careers. Tandy played the rigid Fonsia Dorsey and Cronyn the cantankerous Weller Martin as, in a series of gin games, they revealed unpleasant truths about themselves.

Jack Kroll described their performances as "professionalism raised to the level of incandescence." (Newsweek 10/17/77) For her work in The Gin Game, Tandy received her second Tony Award for Best Actress, another Drama Desk Award, and while on tour Chicago's coveted Sarah Siddons Award (1979) and the Los Angeles Drama Critics Circle Award (1979). Playwright Coburn was awarded the 1978 Pulitzer Prize. The Cronyns also toured with the play to Moscow and Leningrad, under the sponsorship of the U. S. State Department, and then revived the play on London's West End. A videotape of the production, recorded during actual performances in London, was later broadcast on American national public television in June 1980 to widespread acclaim.

In 1981, Tandy accepted a supporting role in Andrew Davies' play Rose, which had been brought to New York from London as a starring vehicle for Glenda Jackson as a maverick British schoolteacher. The production was not a success on Broadway, but Tandy's performance, limited to two scenes, received enthusiastic critical attention and brought her a Tony nomination as best actress in a supporting role. John Simon called Tandy "the most lovable of irritating mothers" and the "most plausible" reason for seeing the play. (New York 4/6/81)

In 1982, the Cronyns appeared together again in the gentle and spirit-affirming Foxfire, inspired by the Foxfire Books, anthologies of anecdotes and interviews collected by high school teacher Elliot Wigginton and his students in southern Appalachia. Susan Cooper and Hume Cronyn fashioned the material into an original stage play that received trial productions at the Stratford Shakespeare Festival in Ontario and the Guthrie Theater in Minneapolis before opening at the Ethel Barrymore Theatre on November 11, 1982.

Critical response to the play was mostly favorable, if not unanimously enthusiastic, but Tandy's performance as the elderly mountain woman Annie Nations confronting a changing world while simultaneously reassessing her own past, was hailed as a consummate achievement. "Everything this actress does is so pure and right that only poets, not theatre critics, should be allowed to write about her," Frank Rich wrote in The New York Times (11/12/82). The performance earned Tandy her third Tony Award for best actress in the nationally-broadcast ceremony, which included a standing ovation from her peers. She also won a Drama Desk Award and another Outer Circle Critics Award to add to her considerable honors.

That same season brought the death of Tennessee Williams. At the playwright's memorial service, held in Broadway's Shubert Theatre, one of the most moving moments for many in the audience occurred as Tandy stepped to the front of the stage, pushed aside the microphone set for the many eulogies, and, thirty-four years after her initial appearance in the play, performed one of Blanche DuBois' speeches from A Streetcar Named Desire. At that moment, not only the playwright and the play but also the actress were memorialized for all time.

The next year Tandy played another Tennessee Williams' character on Broadway: Amanda Wingfield in a revival of The Glass Menagerie directed by John Dexter. The production was generally considered a flawed effort, but her performance was critically esteemed. Frank Rich, celebrating the reunion of Tennessee Williams and Jessica Tandy for the first time in a generation, wrote: "But you pass up Miss Tandy's Amanda Wingfield only at your own peril: You may turn around one day to discover that, in Mr. Williams's phrase, the past has turned into everlasting regret." (The New York Times 12/2/83)

Tandy's more recent appearances have included performances in Louise Page's Salonika at New York's Public Theatre in 1985, a 1985 revival of Foxfire (opposite Cronyn) at the Ahmanson Theatre in Los Angeles and in the televised version in 1987, and in Brian Clark's The Petition in 1986, another two-character play with husband Hume Cronyn at Broadway's Golden Theatre.

The Cronyns, then in their mid-70s, spoke of their performances in The Petition as a valedictory to their theatrical stage team of thirty years. In a New York Times (4/20/86) feature article published five days before The Petition opened, they announced that this would be their last stage performance in a two-character play. Cronyn explained that the rigors of a "two-hander" were too great for actors of their age.

Over the years Tandy continued to work sporatically in films, appearing in September Affair (1950), The Light in the Forest (1958), Adventures of a Young Man (1962), The Birds (1963), and the celebrated Butley (1972) with Alan Bates. In recent years, she has appeared in films with greater frequency and often in tandem with Cronyn. After 1981's little-known Honky Tonk Freeway, David Demby wrote: "Jessica Tandy, eyes glittering with the love of performing after more than 50 years in show business steals the movie in a small role as an alcoholic lady driving to a retirement home with her husband (Hume Cronyn)." (New York 9/7/81) Other recent films include three 1982 releases: Still of the Night, Best Friends, and The World According to Garp. In 1984, she was highly praised for her portrayal of the aged spinster and feminist Miss Birdseye in The Bostonians with Vanessa Redgrave, and she and Cronyn enjoyed critical and popular success in Cocoon (1985) and Batteries Not Included (1987). Of her series of minor film roles she said, "My parts are never big in films, it seems, but that's all right. I'm no longer willing to devote time to developing myself as any sort of presence in Hollywood. Films aren't as satisfying to me as the theater." (The New York Times Magazine 12/26/82)

Then in 1989, at the age of eighty, she became a film star. Tandy accepted the title role in Driving Miss Daisy with Morgan Freeman and won the elusive Academy of Motion Pictures and Sciences ("Oscar") Academy Award for Best Actress as Daisy Werthan in the screen adaptation of Alfred Uhry's successful play. Director Bruce Beresford had resisted casting an actress in the title role who was "not the right age for the role or in easy reach of it." To prepare for the part, Tandy met with Alfred Uhry and talked with him about his family. "I tried very hard to listen to everything about this particular woman," she said. "That was the character I wanted to get to know because she's very individual...." (The New York Times 6/4/89) Tandy received universal praise for creating a third "Southern" woman who retained no traces of Blanche DuBois or of Annie Nations.

Tandy and Cronyn have received joint and separate recognition for their exceptional stage careers. They were both inducted into the Theatre Hall of Fame in 1979. Tandy's other honors have included a Brandeis University Creative Arts Award, an Honorary LL.D. from the University of Western Ontario, and an Honorary L.H.D. from Fordham University in New York City. Tandy was named a recipient of the 1986 annual award by the John F. Kennedy Center for the Performing Arts for "artistic achievement as a performer." In 1990, President George S. Bush in a White House ceremony presented the National Medal of Arts Award to Tandy and Cronyn. Due to illness Tandy was unable to attend the ceremony but Cronyn "stood in" for the two of them.

The Cronyns have made homes in Manhattan, Pound Ridge (Westchester), New York, and Connecticut, since returning to the East coast from Hollywood in the late forties. Today, their principal residence is in Easton, Connecticut. In recent years they have been queried about the longevity of their marriage in a profession where long marriages are the exception rather than the rule. Tandy answered an interviewer from The Washington Post in the following way: "The reason we can live and work together is that in no way do we threaten each other. We're safe: I can't play him and he can't play me. That's basic" (12/23/82).

***

The five feet four inches tall, blue-eyed Jessica Tandy has been esteemed as a preeminent actress of the American theatre since the opening-night of A Streetcar Named Desire on December 3, 1947. The hard work and many years in repertory and the commercial theatre in Britain and the United States were preparatory to the role of Blanche DuBois that thrust her into the annals of American stage history. Her astonishing performance as Tennessee Williams' heroine prepared the way for an artistic achievement that she would sustain in other roles for fifty years.

# Chronology

| | |
|---|---|
| June 7, 1909 | Jessie Alice Tandy was born to Jessie Helen (Horspool) and Harry Tandy in London, England. |
| 1920-1925 | Attended Dame Alice Owen's Girls' School, London. |
| 1924-1927 | Trained for the stage at the Ben Greet Academy of Acting, London. |
| November 22, 1927 | Made professional stage debut as Sara Manderson in <u>The Manderson Girls</u>, Playroom Six, London. |
| April 1928 | Joined the Birmingham Repertory Theatre, England; played Gladys in <u>The Comedy of Good and Evil</u> by Richard Hughes and as Ginevra in <u>Alice Sit-by-the-Fire</u> by J. M. Barrie. |
| | Toured cities in Great Britain as Lydia Blake in <u>Yellow Sands</u> by Eden and Adelaide Phillpotts. |
| February 21, 1929 | Made her London West End debut as Lena Jackson in <u>The Rumour</u> by C. K. Munroe, Court Theatre. |

| | |
|---|---|
| April 5, 1929 | Played the Typist in <u>The Theatre of Life</u>, adapted by George Paston from <u>La Comedie du Bonheur</u> by Nicholas Evreinoff and Fernand Noziere, Arts Theatre, London. |
| June 25, 1929 | Played Maggie in <u>Water</u> by Molly Marshall-Hole, Little Theatre, London. |
| November 10, 1929 | Played The Betrothed in <u>The Unknown Warrior</u> by Cecil Lewis, with Maurice Evans as the Soldier, Arts Theatre, London. |
| March 18, 1930 | Changed professional name from Jessie to Jessica on the advice of producer Lee Shubert. |
| | Made her Broadway debut as Toni Rakonitz in <u>The Matriarch</u> by G. B. Stern and Frank Vernon with Constance Collier in the title role, Longacre Theatre, New York. |
| June 21, 1930 | Played Olivia in <u>Twelfth Night</u> for Oxford University Dramatic Society, England. |
| October 30, 1930 | Played Cynthia Perry in <u>The Last Enemy</u> by Frank Harvey, Shubert Theatre, New York. |
| February 10, 1931 | Played Fay in <u>The Man Who Pays the Piper</u> by G. B. Stern, St. Martin's Theatre, London. |
| April 6, 1931 | Played Audrey in <u>Autumn Crocus</u> by Dodie Smith and C. L. Anthony, Lyric Theatre, London. |
| November 1, 1931 | Played Ruth Blair in <u>Port Said</u> by Emlyn Williams, Wyndham's Theatre, London. |
| November 15, 1931 | Played Anna in <u>Musical Chairs</u> by Ronald Mackenzie with John Gielgud and Margaret Webster, Arts Theatre, London. |

| | |
|---|---|
| 1932 | Married Jack Hawkins, British actor. |
| January 10, 1932 | Played Rita Readle in Below the Surface by J. L. F. Hunt and H. G. Stoker, Repertory Players, London. |
| February 8, 1932 | Played Princess Agnes in Juarez and Maximilian by Franz Werfel, Stage Society, London. |
| April-June 1932 | Performed in repertory in Troilus and Cressida, See Naples and Die, The Witch, Rose Without a Thorn, The Inspector General, The Servant of Two Masters at the Cambridge Festival Theatre, England. |
| July 10, 1932 | Played Carlotta in Mutual Benefit by Roy Jordan, St. Martin's Theatre, London. |
| October 7, 1932 | Played Manuela in Children in Uniform by Christa Winsloe with Cathleen Nesbitt, Duchess Theatre, London. |
| January 22, 1933 | Played Alicia Audley in Lady Audley's Secret by C. H. Hazlewood, Arts Theatre, London. |
| | Made film debut in The Indiscretions of Eve. |
| Spring 1933 | Played Betty Findon in Ten Minute Alibi by Anthony Armstrong, opened January 2, 1933 at Embassy Theatre; Tandy joined the cast for six weeks at the Haymarket Theatre, London. |
| May 21, 1933 | Played Marikke in Midsummer Fires by Hermann Sudermann, Embassy Theatre, London. |
| July 5, 1933 | Played Titania in A Midsummer Night's Dream, Open Air Theatre, Regent's Park, London. |

| | |
|---|---|
| January 1934 | Played in *The Romantic Young Lady*, Fulham Shilling Theatre, England. |
| February 2, 1934 | Played Rosamund in *Birthday*, Cambridge, England. |
| April-May 1934 | Played Viola in *Twelfth Night* and Anne Page in *The Merry Wives of Windsor*, Hippodrome, Manchester, England. |
| August 1934 | Daughter Susan Phyllida Hawkins born. |
| October 24, 1934 | Played Eva Whiston in *Line Engaged* by Jack De Leon and Jack Celestin, Duke of York's Theatre, London. |
| November 14, 1934 | Played Ophelia in *Hamlet* opposite John Gielgud as Hamlet, New Theatre, London. |
| July 2, 1935 | Played Ada in *Noah* by Andre Obey with John Gielgud, New Theatre, London. |
| November 8, 1935 | Played Anna Penn in *Anthony and Anna* by St. John Ervine, Whitehall Theatre, London. |
| August 14, 1936 | Played Marie Rose in *The Ante-Room* by Kate O'Brien, Queen's Theatre, London. |
| November 6, 1936 | Played Jacqueline in *French Without Tears* by Terence Rattigan with Trevor Howard and Rex Harrison, Criterion Theatre, London. |
| December 6, 1936 | Played Pamela March in *Honour Thy Father* by Diana Hamilton, Arts Theatre, London. |
| February 23, 1937 | Played Viola and Sebastian in *Twelfth Night* with Laurence Olivier as Sir Toby Belch and Alec Guinness as Aguecheek, directed by Tyrone Guthrie, Old Vic, London. |

| | |
|---|---|
| April 6, 1937 | Played Katharine in Henry V opposite Laurence Olivier, directed by Tyrone Guthrie, Old Vic, London. |
| June 3, 1937 | Played Ellen Murray in Yes, My Darling Daughter by Mark Reed, St. James's Theatre, London. |
| January 3, 1938 | Played Kay Conway in Time and the Conways by J. B. Priestley with Sybil Thorndike, Ritz Theatre, New York. |
| May 26, 1938 | Played Leda Veerkind in Glorious Morning by Norman Macowan, Duchess Theatre, London. |
| | Appeared in the film, Murder in the Family. |
| January 10, 1939 | Played Nora Fintry in The White Steed by Paul Vincent Carroll with Barry Fitzgerald, Cort Theatre, New York. |
| July 31, 1939 | Played Viola in Twelfth Night, Open Air Theatre, Regent's Park, London. |
| August 28, 1939 | Revival of Twelfth Night, Open Air Theatre, Regent's Park, London. |
| | Toured Canadian cities in Charles the King, Geneva, and Tobias and the Angel. |
| January 30, 1940 | Played Deaconess in Geneva by George Bernard Shaw, Henry Miller's Theatre, New York. |
| April 15, 1940 | Played Cordelia in King Lear with John Gielgud in the title role; directed by Harley Granville-Barker, Old Vic, London. |
| May 29, 1940 | Played Miranda opposite John Gielgud as Prospero in The Tempest, directed by George |

| | |
|---|---|
| | Devine and Marius Goring, Old Vic, London. |
| September 9, 1940 | Played Dr. Mary Murray in *Jupiter Laughs* by A. J. Cronin, Biltmore Theatre, New York. |
| October 7, 1941 | Played Abigail Hill in *Anne of England* by Mary Cass Canfield and Ethel Borden with Flora Robson and Leo G. Carroll, St. James Theatre, New York. |
| 1942 | Divorced Jack Hawkins and settled permanently in the United States. |
| April 14, 1942 | Played Cattrin in *Yesterday's Magic* by Emlyn Williams, Guild Theatre, New York. |
| September 27, 1942 | Married Hume Cronyn and settled in Hollywood. |
| July 22, 1943 | Son Christopher Hume Cronyn born in California. |
| 1944 | Appeared with Spencer Tracy and Hume Cronyn in first Hollywood film, *The Seventh Cross*. |
| 1945 | Appeared with Greer Garson and Gregory Peck in the film, *The Valley of Decision*. |
| November 26, 1945 | Daughter Tandy Cronyn born in California. |
| 1946 | Appeared with Charles Coburn and Hume Cronyn in the film, *The Green Years*. |
| | Appeared with Gene Tierney and Vincent Price in the film, *Dragonwyck*. |
| January 1946 | Played Miss Lucretia Collins in *Portrait of a Madonna* by Tennessee Williams, directed by Hume Cronyn, Actors' Laboratory Theatre, Las Palmas Theatre, Los Angeles. |

| | |
|---|---|
| | Cast as Blanche DuBois in *A Streetcar Named Desire*. |
| 1947 | Appeared with Linda Darnelle and Cornell Wilde in the film, *Forever Amber*. |
| October 6, 1947 | Began rehearsals for *A Streetcar Named Desire*. |
| November 1947 | Tryouts for *A Streetcar Named Desire* in New Haven, Boston, and Philadelphia. |
| December 3, 1947 | Opened as Blanche DuBois in *A Streetcar Named Desired*, directed by Elia Kazan, on Broadway, Ethel Barrymore Theatre, New York. She performed the role on Broadway for over two years. |
| 1948 | Appeared with Charles Boyer and Ann Blyth in the film, *A Woman's Vengeance*. |
| | Served as Dramatic Adviser to the Goddard Neighborhood Center, New York. |
| March 1948 | Won 1947 Antoinette Perry ("Tony") Award for Best Actress as Blanche DuBois in *A Streetcar Named Desire*. |
| July 22, 1949 | Performed in world premiere of *Now I Lay Me Down to Sleep* by Elaine Ryan, directed by Hume Cronyn, Stanford University's Memorial Auditorium. |
| August 14, 1950 | Played with Hume Cronyn in *The Little Blue Light* by Edmund Wilson, Brattle Theatre, Cambridge, MA. |
| | Appeared with Joan Fontaine and Joseph Cotton in the film, *September Affair*. |
| November 1, 1950 | Played title role in *Hilda Crane* by Samson Raphaelson, directed by Hume Cronyn, Coronet Theatre, New York. |

| | |
|---|---|
| 1951 | Lost film role of Blanche DuBois to Vivien Leigh. |
| | Appeared with James Mason in the film, The Desert Fox. |
| October 24, 1951 | Played Agnes in The Fourposter by Jan de Hartog with Hume Cronyn, Ethel Barrymore Theatre, New York. |
| 1952 | Became a naturalized U. S. citizen. |
| February 23, 1953 | Played The Fourposter at the Royal Alexandra Theatre, Toronto, on tour. |
| December 1, 1953 | Played Mary Doyle in a revival of Madam, Will You Walk by Sidney Howard with Hume Cronyn, Phoenix Theatre, New York. |
| September-December 1954 | Toured cities in the United States with Cronyn in Face to Face, a concert reading of poetry and prose ranging from Shakespeare to Ogden Nash. |
| January 5, 1955 | Played Agnes in revival of The Fourposter with Hume Cronyn, City Center, New York. |
| September 26, 1955 | Played Frances Farrar in A Day By the Sea by N. C. Hunter with Hume Cronyn, ANTA Playhouse, New York. |
| Summer 1957 | Toured U. S. cities with Cronyn in The Man in the Dogsuit. |
| April 28, 1958 | Played Mary in The Honeys by Roald Dahl with Hume Cronyn, Longacre Theatre, New York. |
| Summer 1958 | Toured U. S. cities in Triple Play, three one-acts by Tennessee Williams and Sean O'Casey. |

| | |
|---|---|
| October 30, 1958 | Played Martha Walling in The Man in the Dog Suit by Albert Belch and William H. Wright with Hume Cronyn, Coronet Theatre, New York. |
| | Appeared with James MacArthur and Carol Lynley in the film, The Light in the Forest. |
| April 15, 1959 | Performed in Triple Play as Miss Lucretia Collins in Portrait of a Madonna by Tennessee Williams, Angela Nightingale in Bedtime Story and the Innocent Bystander in Pound on Demand by Sean O'Casey, directed by Hume Cronyn, Playhouse, New York. |
| December 2, 1959 | Played Louise Harrington in Five Finger Exercise by Peter Shaffer, directed by John Gielgud, Music Box Theatre, New York. |
| 1960-1961 | Performed in National Tour of Five Finger Exercise. |
| April 1960 | Became a member of the Theatre Advisory Group to the Hopkins Center at Dartmouth College, Hanover, New Hampshire. |
| June 17, 1961 | Played Lady Macbeth in Macbeth with Pat Hingle in title role, American Shakespeare Festival Theatre, Stratford, CT. |
| July 23, 1961 | Played Cassandra in Troilus and Cressida, American Shakespeare Festival Theatre, Stratford, CT. |
| September 18, 1962 | Played Edith Maitland opposite Hume Cronyn in Big Fish, Little Fish by Hugh Wheeler, Duke of York's Theatre, London. |
| | Appeared with Richard Beymer in the film, Adventures of a Young Man. |

| | |
|---|---|
| 1963 | Joined Tyrone Guthrie's Minnesota Theatre Company, Minneapolis, for its first season. |
| May 7, 1963 | Played Gertrude in <u>Hamlet</u>, directed by Tyrone Guthrie, The Guthrie Theater, Minneapolis. |
| June 18, 1963 | Played Olga in <u>The Three Sisters</u> by Anton Chekhov, The Guthrie Theater, Minneapolis. |
| July 16, 1963 | Played Linda Loman in <u>Death of a Salesman</u> by Arthur Miller opposite Hume Cronyn, The Guthrie Theater, Minneapolis. |
| April 1964 | Appeared with Rod Taylor and Tippi Hedren in the film, <u>The Birds</u>. |
| October 13, 1964 | Played Doktor Mathilde van Zahnd in <u>The Physicists</u> by Friedrich Duerrenmatt, Martin Beck Theatre, New York. |
| May 11, 1965 | Played Lady Wishfort in <u>The Way of the World</u> by William Congreve, The Guthrie Theater, Minneapolis. |
| June 15, 1965 | Played Madame Ranevskaya in <u>The Cherry Orchard</u> by Anton Chekhov, directed by Tyrone Guthrie, The Guthrie Theater, Minneapolis. |
| August 3, 1965 | Appeared in the Prologue of <u>The Caucasian Chalk Circle</u> by Bertolt Brecht, The Guthrie Theater, Minneapolis. |
| 1965 | Performed readings in "Hear America Speaking," White House, Washington, D.C. |
| September 12, 1966 | Played Agnes in <u>A Delicate Balance</u> by Edward Albee with Hume Cronyn and directed by Alan Schneider, Martin Beck Theatre, New York. |

| | |
|---|---|
| 1967 | Played Agnes in the National Touring Company of A Delicate Balance. |
| 1968 | Played Frosine in The Miser by Moliere with Hume Cronyn, Center Theatre Group at the Mark Taper Forum, Los Angeles, CA. |
| July 5, 1968 | Played Hesione Hushabye in Heartbreak House by George Bernard Shaw, Shaw Festival, Niagara-on-the-Lake, Ontario, Canada. |
| 1969 | Played Pamela Pew-Pickett in Tchin-Tchin, Ivanhoe Theatre, Chicago, IL. |
| January 8, 1970 | Played Marguerite Gautier in Camino Real by Tennessee Williams, The Repertory Theatre of Lincoln Center, Vivian Beaumont Theatre, New York. |
| January-February 1971 | Played Marjorie in Home by David Storey with John Gielgud, Ralph Richardson and Mona Washbourne, Morosco Theatre, New York. |
| March 27, 1971 | Played The Wife in All Over by Edward Albee with Colleen Dewhurst, directed by Alan Schneider, Martin Beck Theatre, New York. |
| June 1971 | Became a founding member of Solar Theater, Inc., a non-profit producing group located in Manhattan. |
| 1972-1973 | Toured in Promenade All by David E. Robison with Hume Cronyn. |
| August 1972 | Traveled to Paris with Alan Schneider and Barney Rossett, Beckett's American publisher, to talk with Samuel Beckett about a new play for the Beckett Festival--Not I. |

| | |
|---|---|
| November 20, 1972 | Played Winnie in Happy Days by Samuel Beckett with Hume Cronyn, directed by Alan Schneider, for Beckett Festival, Forum Theatre at Lincoln Center, New York. Cronyn also appeared in Act Without Words 1. |
| November 22, 1972 | Played Mouth in Not I by Samuel Beckett, directed by Alan Schneider, for Beckett Festival, Forum Theatre at Lincoln Center, New York. |
| 1973 | Received 1973 Village Voice Off-Broadway ("Obie") Award for Best Actress in Not I. |
| | Toured U. S. campuses as the Mouth in Not I and Winnie in Happy Days. |
| 1974-1975 | Toured U.S. cities in The Many Faces of Love, concert readings. |
| January 1974 | Appeared with Alan Bates in the film Butley. |
| February 24, 1974 | Played Anna-May Conklin in Come into the Garden Maude and Hilde Latymer in A Song at Twilight in Noel Coward in Two Keys, with Hume Cronyn and Anne Baxter, Ethel Barrymore Theatre, New York. |
| | Received honorary L.L.D., University of Western Ontario, Canada. |
| February 17, 1975 | Performed in National Touring Company of Noel Coward in Two Keys. |
| 1976 | Performed in The Many Faces of Love, concert readings, Theatre London, Ontario, Canada. |
| June 7, 1976 | Played Lady Wishfort in The Way of the World, Hippolyta/Titania in A Midsummer Night's Dream, and the title role in Eve, |

| | |
|---|---|
| | Stratford Shakespeare Festival Theatre, Ontario, Canada. |
| 1977 | Played Mary Tyrone in Long Day's Journey into Night by Eugene O'Neill, directed by Robin Phillips, Theatre London, Ontario, Canada. |
| October 6, 1977 | Played Fonsia Dorsey opposite Hume Cronyn in The Gin Game by D. L. Coburn, directed by Mike Nichols, Golden Theatre, New York. |
| March 1978 | Won 1977 Antoinette Perry ("Tony") Award for Best Actress as Fonsia Dorsey in The Gin Game. |
| October 5, 1978-June 10, 1979 | Performed in tour of The Gin Game to cities in the United States, Canada, and in the U.S.S.R. |
| 1979 | Inducted into Theatre Hall of Fame. |
| July 21, 1979 | Performed in the revival of The Gin Game, Lyric Theatre, London. |
| 1980 | Played Annie Nations in Foxfire, an original play by Susan Cooper and Hume Cronyn, and Mary Tyrone in Long Day's Journey into Night by Eugene O'Neill, Stratford Shakespeare Festival Theatre, Ontario, Canada. |
| March 26, 1981 | Played Mother in Rose by Andrew Davies with Glenda Jackson in the title role, Cort Theatre, New York. |
| August 1981 | Appeared with Hume Cronyn in the film, Honky Tonk Freeway. |
| 1982 | Played Annie Nations in Foxfire, directed by Marshall W. Mason, The Guthrie Theatre, Minneapolis. |

| | |
|---|---|
| July 1982 | Appeared with Robin Williams and Glenn Close in the film, The World According to Garp. |
| November 11, 1982 | Played Annie Nations in Foxfire with Hume Cronyn, Ethel Barrymore Theatre, New York. |
| December 1982 | Appeared with Roy Scheider and Meryl Streep in the film, Still of the Night. |
| | Appeared with Burt Reynolds and Goldie Hawn in the film, Best Friends. |
| March 1983 | Won 1982 Antoinette Perry ("Tony") Award for Best Actress as Annie Nations in Foxfire. |
| | Received The Common Wealth Award for Distinguished Service in Dramatic Arts. |
| December 1, 1983 | Played Amanda Wingfield in The Glass Menagerie by Tennessee Williams, directed by John Dexter, Eugene O'Neill Theatre, New York. |
| July 1984 | Appeared with Vanessa Redgrave and Christopher Reeves in the film, The Bostonians. |
| April 2, 1985 | Played Charlotte in Salonika by Louise Page, New York Shakespeare Festival Public Theatre, New York. |
| | Received L.H.D. from Fordham University, New York. |
| June 1985 | Appeared with Hume Cronyn in the film Cocoon. |
| | Performed in revival of Foxfire with Hume Cronyn, directed by David Trainer, Ahmanson Theatre, Los Angeles. |

| | |
|---|---|
| April 24, 1986 | Played Lady Elisabeth Milne opposite Hume Cronyn in The Petition by Brian Clark, Golden Theatre, New York. |
| | Nominated for Best Actress in The Petition at the Antoinette Perry ("Tony") Awards. |
| | Received with Cronyn The John F. Kennedy Center Honors Award for the Arts. |
| 1987 | Appeared with Hume Cronyn in the film Batteries Not Included. |
| | Received Alley Theatre Award for Significant Contributions to Theatre Arts, Houston. |
| | Received Academy of Science Fiction, Fantasy, and Horror Films Award for Best Actress for Batteries not Included. |
| | Appeared in the Hallmark Hall of Fame television production of Foxfire with the Broadway cast. |
| March 1988 | Appeared with Kelly McGillis in the film The House on Carroll Street. |
| | Appeared with Cronyn in the film Cocoon: The Return. |
| | Received with Hume Cronyn the American Academy of Dramatic Arts Franklin Haven Sargent Award for Outstanding Quality of Acting. |
| | Received an Emmy Award for Best Dramatic Actress in a Television Special for Foxfire. |
| December 1989 | Appeared in the title role with Morgan Freeman in the film Driving Miss Daisy. |

| | |
|---|---|
| March 26, 1990 | Won the 1989 Academy of Motion Pictures and Sciences ("Oscar") Award for Best Actress in Driving Miss Daisy. |
| May 10, 1990 | Received with Hume Cronyn and other American artists the National Medal of Arts Award presented by President George Bush in the East Room of the White House. |
| 1991 | Theatre LA Annual Ovation Award to artists demonstrating a long-term commitment to theatre in Los Angeles. Also to Hume Cronyn. |
| June 1991 | Filmed The Story Lady for NBC-TV with daughter Tandy Cronyn. Jessica Tandy appeared in title role. |

# Stage Appearances

## The Early Years
## 1927-1946

**S01** The Manderson Girls (Playroom Six, London; November 22, 1927) Jessie Tandy made her professional stage debut as Sara Manderson.

**S02** The Comedy of Good and Evil and Alice Sit-by-the-Fire (Birmingham Repertory Theatre, England; 1928) Tandy played two ingenue roles as Gladys in Richard Hughes' The Comedy of Good and Evil and as Ginevra in J. M. Barrie's Alice Sit-by-the-Fire.

**S03** Yellow Sands by Eden and Adelaide Phillpotts (Birmingham Repertory Theatre on tour; 1928) Tandy played Lydia Blake.

**S04** The Rumour (Court Theatre, London; February 21, 1929) Tandy made her West End debut in London as Lena Jackson in the play by C. K. Monroe. This was the first of a series of West End performances for Tandy.

**S05** The Theatre of Life (Arts Theatre, London; April 5, 1929) Tandy played the Typist in George Paston's play, adapted from La Comedie du Bonheur by Nicholas Evreinoff and Fernand Noziere, in the West End.

**S06** Water (Little Theatre, London; June 25, 1929) Tandy played Maggie in the play by Molly Marshall-Hole.

**S07** The Unknown Warrior (Arts Theatre, London; November 10, 1929) Tandy played The Betrothed in the play by Cecil Lewis with Maurice Evans as The Soldier.

**S08** The Matriarch (Longacre Theatre, Broadway; March 18, 1930) G. B. Stern's play featured Constance Collier as "The Matriarch" and Jessica Tandy as Tony Rakonitz, her granddaughter. This was Tandy's first role on Broadway and her first role performed under her new stage name--Jessica Tandy.

**S09** Twelfth Night (Oxford University Dramatic Society, England; June 21, 1930) Tandy appeared as Olivia in her first Shakespearean role.

**S10** The Last Enemy (Shubert Theatre, Broadway; October 30, 1930) Tandy played Cynthia Perry in Frank Harvey's play with a British cast. She was praised by the New York Times reviewer for her "simple, direct acting."

**S11** The Man Who Pays the Piper (St. Martin's Theatre, London; February 10, 1931) Tandy was cast as Fay in G. B. Stern's play.

**S12** Autumn Crocus (Lyric Theatre, London; April 6, 1931) Tandy played Audrey in the play by Dodie Smith and C. L Anthony in the London production.

**S13** Port Said (Wyndham's Theatre, London; November 1, 1931) Tandy played Ruth Blair in the play by Emlyn Williams with Jack Hawkins and Emlyn Williams in the cast.

**S14** Musical Chairs (Arts Theatre, London; November 15, 1931) Ronald Mackenzie's play, directed by Theodore Komissarjevsky, featured John Gielgud, Frank Vosper, Finlay Currie, Margaret Webster, and Tandy in the cast.

**S15** Below the Surface (Repertory Players, London; January 10, 1932) Tandy played Rita Readle in the play by J. L. F. Hunt and H. G. Stoker with Jack Hawkins in the cast.

**S16** Juarez and Maximilian (Stage Society, London; February 8, 1932) Tandy played Princess Agnes in Franz Werfel's play with English version by Ruth Langner.

**S17** Troilus and Cressida, See Naples and Die, The Witch, Rose Without a Thorn, The Inspector General, The Servant of Two Masters (Cambridge Festival Theatre,

England; April-June 1932) Tandy played in repertory with the Cambridge Festival Theatre.

**S18** Mutual Benefit (St. Martin's Theatre, London; July 10, 1932) Tandy played Carlotta in Roy Jordan's play.

**S19** Children in Uniform (Duchess Theatre, London; October 7, 1932) Tandy played Manuela, the young schoolgirl, in Christa Winsloe's play with Cathleen Nesbitt as the headmistress. The London Times cited Tandy as a "distinguished young actress."

**S20** Ten Minute Alibi (Haymarket Theatre, London; January 2, 1933) Tandy played Betty Findon, replacing Maisie Darrel, after the play by Anthony Armstrong moved from the Embassy Theatre to the Haymarket in February.

**S21** Lady Audley's Secret (Arts Theatre, London; January 22, 1933) Tandy played Alicia Audley with Flora Robson as Lady Audley in the play by C. H. Hazlewood.

**S22** Midsummer Fires (Embassy Theatre, London; May 21, 1933) Tandy played Marikke in the play by Hermann Sudermann with Eric Portman in the cast.

**S23** A Midsummer Night's Dream (Open Air Theatre, London; July 5, 1933) Tandy was seen as Titania.

**S24** The Romantic Young Lady (Fulham Shilling Theatre, England; January 1934)

**S25** Birthday (Cambridge, England; February 2, 1934) Tandy played Rosamund.

**S26** Twelfth Night, The Merry Wives of Windsor (Hippodrome, Manchester, England; April-May 1934) Tandy appeared in repertory as Viola in Twelfth Night and as Anne Page in The Merry Wives of Windsor.

**S27** Line Engaged (Duke of York's Theatre, London; October 24, 1934) Tandy played Eva Whiston in the play by Jack De Leon and Jack Celestin.

**S28** Hamlet (New Theatre, London; November 14, 1934) Tandy appeared as Ophelia opposite John Gielgud as Hamlet with Jack Hawkins as Horatio, Frank Vosper as Claudius, Glen Byam Shaw as Laertes, and Alec Guinness as Osric. Anthony Quayle and George Devine were also in the cast. This production made the young John Gielgud a Shakespearean star.

**S29** Noah (New Theatre, London; July 2, 1935) Tandy played Ada in Andre Obey's play with John Gielgud as Noah.

**S30** Anthony and Anna (Whitehall Theatre, London; November 8, 1935) Tandy played Anna Penn in the play by St. John Ervine.

**S31** The Ante-Room (Queen's Theatre, London; August 14, 1936) Tandy played Marie Rose in the play by Kate O'Brien.

**S32** French Without Tears (Criterion Theatre, London; November 6, 1936) Tandy apppeared as Jacqueline opposite Trevor Howard and Rex Harrison in Terence Rattigan's play.

**S33** Honour Thy Father (Arts Theatre, London; December 6, 1936) Tandy played Pamela March in a play by Diana Hamilton.

**S34** Twelfth Night (Old Vic, London; February 23, 1937) Tandy appeared as Viola and Sebastian opposite Laurence Olivier as Sir Toby Belch and Alec Guinness as Aguecheek. The production was directed by Tyrone Guthrie.

**S35** Henry V (Old Vic, London; April 6, 1937) Tandy appeared opposite Laurence Olivier in the title role. These performances in repertory at the Old Vic in the 1937 season established Olivier as a rising star on the London theatre scene and Tandy as a distinguished young actress.

**S36** Yes, My Darling Daughter (St. James's Theatre, London; June 3, 1937) Tandy played Ellen Murray in Mark Reed's play.

**S37** Time and the Conways (Ritz Theatre, Broadway; January 3, 1938) J. B. Priestley's play was staged with Sybil Thorndike as Mrs. Conway and Tandy as her daughter Kay. This was Tandy's second appearance on Broadway following The Matriarch. The New York Times reviewer praised Tandy for acting the part with "the lucidity and spirit of an actress who has mastered her role."

**S38** Glorious Morning (Duchess Theatre, London; May 26, 1938) Tandy played Leda Veerkind in Norman Macowan's play.

**S39** The White Steed (Cort Theatre, New York; January 10, 1939) Tandy played Nora Fintry in Paul Vincent Carroll's play starring Barry Fitzgerald and directed by Hugh Hunt.

**S40** Twelfth Night (Open Air Theatre, Regent's Park, London; July 31, 1939 and August 28, 1939) Tandy appeared as Viola.

**S41** Charles the King, Geneva, and Tobias and The Angel (Canada; 1939) Tandy toured Canadian cities in these three plays.

**S42** Geneva (Henry Miller's Theatre, Broadway; January 30, 1940) George Bernard Shaw's play, first produced in 1938, came to Broadway after its Canadian tour. Tandy had the small part of the Deaconess.

**S43** King Lear (Old Vic, London; April 15, 1940) Tandy played Cordelia with Fay Compton and Cathleen Nesbitt as Lear's other daughters and John Gielgud in the title role. The production was directed by Harley Granville-Barker.

**S44** The Tempest (Old Vic, London; May 29, 1940) Tandy appeared as Miranda opposite John Gielgud as Prospero with Marius Goring as Ariel. The production was directed by George Devine and Marius Goring.

**S45** Jupiter Laughs (Biltmore Theatre, Broadway; September 9, 1940) Tandy played Dr. Mary Murray with Alexander Knox in A. J. Cronin's play. Tandy was praised by The Times for her lucidity of style and personal beauty.

**S46** Anne of England (St. James Theatre, Broadway; October 7, 1941) Tandy played Abigail Hill opposite Flora Robson and Leo G. Carroll in the historical play by Mary Cass Canfield and Ethel Borden.

**S47** Yesterday's Magic (Guild Theatre, Broadway; April 14, 1942) Tandy played Cattrin with Paul Muni in Emlyn Williams' play produced by the Theatre Guild.

**S48** Portrait of a Madonna (Actors' Laboratory Theatre, Los Angeles; January 1946) Tandy appeared as Miss Lucretia Collins in Tennessee Williams' one-act play, directed by Hume Cronyn. Her performance in a revival staged in the summer won her the role of Blanche DuBois in a new Williams' play being cast for Broadway production.

## The Broadway Years
## 1947-1986

**S49** **A Streetcar Named Desire** (1947)

**Credits**

Play by Tennessee Williams

| | |
|---|---|
| Producer | Irene M. Selznick |
| Director | Elia Kazan |
| Scenery and Lighting | Jo Mielziner |
| Costume Designer | Lucinda Ballard |

**Cast**

| | |
|---|---|
| Blanche DuBois | Jessica Tandy |
| Stanley Kowalski | Marlon Brando |
| Harold Mitchell (Mitch) | Karl Malden |
| Stella Kowalski | Kim Hunter |
| Negro Woman | Gee Gee James |
| Eunice Hubbel | Peg Hillias |
| Steve Hubbel | Rudy Bond |
| Pablo Gonzales | Nick Dennis |
| A Young Collector | Vito Christi |
| Mexican Woman | Edna Thomas |
| A Strange Woman | Ann Dere |
| A Strange Man | Richard Garrick |

**The Play's History**

A Streetcar Named Desire opened on December 3, 1947 at the Ethel Barrymore Theatre.

**Synopsis**

Blanche DuBois arrives at the New Orleans tenement home of Stella and Stanley Kowalski, her pregnant sister and Polish brother-in-law. Blanche's faded Southern gentility clashes with Stanley's brutish masculinity. She seeks protection from a harsh world and she competes with Stanley for Stella's affections but finds herself no match for his sexual hold over her sister. She tries to charm the lonely Mitch, Stanley's poker-playing friend, into marrying her. However, Stanley destroys Blanche's hopes for marriage (and refuge) by telling Mitch about her past drunkenness and promiscuity in Laurel, Mississippi. As Stella reproaches Stanley for his cruelty, her labor pains begin and Stanley rushes her to the hospital.

Blanche is visited by a drunken Mitch, who accuses her of lying to him and makes a pathetic effort to seduce her. He finally insults her and leaves. Stanley returns to find Blanche dressed for a party, fantasizing about an invitation to go on a cruise with a wealthy friend. Angered by her pretensions, Stanley starts a fight with her that ends in rape. In a final scene some weeks later,

Blanche, her tenuous hold on reality shattered, is taken to a mental hospital.

**Commentary**

A Streetcar Named Desire was Tennessee Williams' second play produced on Broadway within a year (The Glass Menagerie opened on March 31, 1946). A Streetcar Named Desire established Williams as America's premier playwright and Jessica Tandy and Marlon Brando, both newcomers to the Broadway stage, as stars. The casting of Tandy in the role of Blanche DuBois came after a long and arduous search by director, producer, and playwright. After seeing Tandy in a production of Portrait of a Madonna in Los Angeles (directed by Hume Cronyn), Kazan, Selznick, and Williams agreed that they had found "Blanche."

**Reviews**

New York Times (12-4-47)--The Times reviewer, Brooks Atkinson, hailed Streetcar as a masterpiece, calling it a "perfect marriage of acting and playwriting." He called Jessica Tandy's performance as Williams' rueful heroine "superb." "Miss Tandy is a trim, agile actress," he wrote, "with a lovely voice and quick intelligence." Atkinson praised the playwright's poetic imagination, compassion, and luminous story.

New York Times (12-14-47)--Atkinson's second review of Streetcar appeared ten days after the first. Acknowledging that the play was the finest new play on Broadway and a "smash hit," Atkinson proceeded to analyze Williams' accomplishment. The playwright did not address great social issues, solved no problems and arrived at no general moral conclusions. Nor did he deal with "representative" men and women. Instead, Williams established a "rare and wonderful" presence of truth supported by extraordinary acting and directing. "As Blanche DuBois," Atkinson wrote in this lengthy piece, "Jessica Tandy has one of the longest and most exacting parts on record." "She plays it with an insight so vibrant and pitiless. . . for she catches on the wing the terror, the bogus refinement, the intellectual alertness and the madness that can hardly be distinguished from logic and fastidiousness. Miss Tandy acts a magnificant part magnificently."

*****

**S50** **Hilda Crane** (1950)

**Credits**

Play by Samson Raphaelson
Producer Arthur Schwartz

| | |
|---|---|
| Director | Hume Cronyn |
| Scenic Designer | Howard Bay |
| Costumes | Bergdorf Goodman and Harriett Ames |
| Production Assistant | Victor Samrock |

**Cast**

| | |
|---|---|
| Hilda Crane | Jessica Tandy |
| Clara | Ann Sullivan |
| Henry Ottwell | John Alexander |
| Mrs. Crane | Beulah Bondi |
| Mrs. Ottwell | Evelyn Varden |
| Prof. Charles Jensen | Frank Sundstrom |
| Neil Bromley | Eileen Heckart |
| Dink Bromley | Richard McMurray |
| Mrs. Nordinger | Madeleine King |
| Mr. Nordinger | Watson White |
| Miss Keavney | Frieda Altman |

**The Play's History**

Hilda Crane opened on November 1, 1950 at the Coronet Theatre. At the time the play opened, Samson Raphaelson was best known for The Jazz Singer (1925), a highly successful comedy starring George Jessel.

**Synopsis**

Hilda Crane is about the plight of the independent-minded woman in contemporary society. Hilda returns to her native Winona, Illinois, after failures in New York business and in two marriages. Back home, she is loved by two men. One is an honorable but dull lawnmower manufacturer and the other a morally-dubious college professor. The businessman's mother is unpleasant and possessive and attempts to prevent her son from marrying Hilda. Hilda's own mother urges her to marry for comfort and security in order to find happiness.

For two years after her marriage to the manufacturer, Hilda tries to conform to her husband's standards but finds her existence stifling. She meets the professor again and commits adultery to escape boredom, thus wrecking her third marriage. Realizing that she is little better than a "tramp," she takes an overdose of sleeping pills and dies.

**Commentary**

Critics compared Hilda Crane to A Streetcar Named Desire because of the misfit heroines who fail to adjust their twisted emotional lives to the world about them. Tandy's effort to find another leading role was often dismissed as just another neurotic role for the heroine of A Streetcar Named Desire.

**Reviews**
New York Times (11-2-50)--Hilda Crane, according to the Times reviewer, is admirably acted by Jessica Tandy in the role of a tiresome egotist but in a play lacking in originality. Since the title character is always on the verge of insanity, Brooks Atkinson makes the unavoidable comparison between Hilda Crane and Blanche DuBois played by Tandy two years earlier, though the Raphaelson character is more commonplace and in a more conventional drama.

*****

**S51** **The Fourposter** (1951)

**Credits**
Play by Jan de Hartog

| | |
|---|---|
| Producers | The Playwrights Company |
| Director | Jose Ferrer |
| Scene Designer | Syrjala |
| Costume Designer | Lucinda Ballard |

**Cast**

| | |
|---|---|
| Agnes | Jessica Tandy |
| Michael | Hume Cronyn |

**The Play's History**
The Fourposter opened October 24, 1951 at the Ethel Barrymore Theatre and ran for 632 performances.

**Synopsis**
Hartog's comedy is the story of thirty-five years in the married life of Agnes and Michael. The two-character play takes its title from a huge, ornate bed with a tester that changes with the decades. In 1890, the couple enters the spare bedroom in Michael's house as bride and groom. He carries Agnes across the threshold of the bedroom as the play begins. In the next few years they have a son and daughter. Ten years later Michael is prevented from losing his head over another woman. Their offspring marry and leave them alone. In 1925, Michael and Agnes sell the house, pack-up, and leave.

**Commentary**
The play established Tandy and Cronyn as an acting team.

**Reviews**
New York Times (10-25-51)--Reviewer Brooks Atkinson calls The Fourposter the "most civilized comedy we have had on marriage for years." In praise of the extraordinary acting, the reviewer observes that Jessica Tandy skims lightly through the follies and crises of Agnes' married life with "interior restlessness and fury." In the part of Michael, Cronyn gives a "capital performance" that is entertaining in its swings from rapture to anxiety to petulance to bewilderment.

*****

**S52** The Honeys (1955)

**Credits**

| | |
|---|---|
| Play by Roald Dahl | |
| Producer | Cheryl Crawford |
| Director | Frank Corsaro |
| Scenic Designer | Ben Edwards |
| Costume Designer | Motley |

**Cast**

| | |
|---|---|
| Maggie | Dorothy Stickney |
| Mary | Jessica Tandy |
| Curtis Honey | Hume Cronyn |
| Bennett Honey | Hume Cronyn |
| Nellie Fleischman | Mary Finney |
| Potts | Dana Elcar |

**The Play's History**

The Honeys opened on April 28, 1955 at the Longacre Theatre.

**Synopsis**

Inspired by a friend who lost her husband when he fell from a window and tells tales of her travels and experiences, the two sisters-in-law, Maggie and Mary Honey, decide they can dispense with their humiliations and live rich, full lives if only they were rid of their husbands. Bennett Honey thinks the height of excitement is shuffleboard in St. Petersburg and his gluttonous twin brother Curtis buys animal heads at auctions because he is too frightened to go hunting. The wives plot to exterminate their husbands. In one way or another they maneuver their mates to their demise.

Having heard that oysters can be poisonous if properly treated, they manage to feed them to one of the husbands. The other husband, after escaping from a locked elevator, meets his end in a scuffle in which his wife hits him with a leg of lamb.

**Commentary**

The comparison with Joseph Kesselring's Arsenic and Old Lace, a comedy about two charming and innocent women who populate their cellar with the remains of "acceptable" roomers, was inevitable.

**Reviews**

New York Times (4-29-55)--Though a farce about a pair of wives who decide to do in their cantankerous husbands who are twin brothers, The Honey's for reviewer Lewis Funke is not sufficiently demented to be in the same class as Arsenic and Old Lace. As the twin brothers, Cronyn gives a "first-rate" performance. As the devoted and long-suffering wife, Tandy is effective as she divests herself of her loyalty and decides "to head for widowhood."

*****

**S53** **The Man in the Dog Suit** (1958)

**Credits**

| | |
|---|---|
| Play by Albert Belch and William H. Wright | |
| Producers | The Producers Theatre |
| Associate Producer | Lewis Allen |
| Director | Ralph Nelson |
| Scenic & Lighting Designer | Donald Oenslager |
| Costume Designer | Anna Hill Johnstone |
| Associate Producer | Lewis Allen |
| Production Stage Manager | Paul A. Foley |

**Cast**

| | |
|---|---|
| Martha Walling | Jessica Tandy |
| Oliver Walling | Hume Cronyn |
| Letty Gaxton | Nancy Cushman |
| Henry Gaxton | John McGovern |
| George Stoddard | John Griggs |
| Eileen Stoddard | Carmen Mathews |
| Mrs. Louisa Stoddard | Kathleen Comegys |
| Stewart Stoddard | Clinton Sundberg |
| Anthony Roberti | Tom Carlin |
| Mr. Beal | Arthur Hughes |

**The Play's History**

Adapted from the novel by Edwin Corle, The Man in the Dog Suit opened on October 30, 1958 at the Coronet Theatre.

**Synopsis**

The Man in the Dog Suit is the familiar story of an unhappy bank clerk who dreams of a wonderful life in the woods of the great Northwest and feels happy and free only when he wears a dog-suit which he acquired for a masquerade ball. He continues to wear the dog-suit, his symbol of freedom, whenever he feels depressed. His gaucheries infuriate his wife's rich family who just happen to own the bank where he is employed. They create complications but their most insufferable member is a crook whose illegal ventures are discovered and bravely thwarted by the man in the dog-suit.

**Commentary**

This is the first of several stage plays and films that raised the question in the long careers of Hume Cronyn and Jessica Tandy about their choice of mediocre material. They have answered the question over the years by saying that it is important to keep working and that good material does not always present itself, especially in the commercial theatre.

**Reviews**

New York Times (10-31-58)--Brooks Atkinson, writing for the Times, asks the penetrating question: Why do the Cronyns waste their talent on such mediocre nonsense? Reviewed as a mechanical piece, Atkinson puzzles upon the Cronyns choice of material on which to "squander" their talents.

*****

**S54** **Five Finger Exercise** (1959)

**Credits**

Play by Peter Shaffer

| | |
|---|---|
| Producers | Frederick Brisson and the Playwrights Company |
| Director | John Gielgud |
| Scene Designer | Oliver Smith |
| Lighting Designer | Tharon Musser |
| Production Stage Manager | Fred Hebert |

**Cast**

| | |
|---|---|
| Louise Harrington | Jessica Tandy |
| Stanley Harrington | Roland Culver |
| Clive Harrington | Brian Bedford |
| Pamela Harrington | Juliet Mills |
| Walter Langer | Michael Bryant |

**The Play's History**

Five Finger Exercise opened December 2, 1959 at the Music Box Theatre and ran for 337 performances.

**Synopsis**

The play is a study of family relationships within a British home. The weekend country house of the Harringtons in Suffolk is luxuriously furnished. Beneath the civilized surface of their lives, there is rancor and hatred. The mother is a cultural snob and the father is common.

As part of the family's social pretentiousness, the mother engages a German young man to live with the family and tutor the adolescent daughter. Since no one in the family can communicate freely, they turn their frustrations toward him. Bit by bit pressure builds up and explodes in what promises to be a grisly catastrophe in the last scene. Everyone is shocked, but there is no certainty that the future will be much brighter.

**Commentary**

Five Finger Exercise opened the previous season in London and continued to play in the West End with a new cast while the original British cast, with the addition of Jessica Tandy, transferred to Broadway.

**Reviews**

New York Times (12-3-1959)--Describing Five Finger Exercise as a play not so much written as lived, reviewer Brooks Atkinson praises the underwriting of Peter Shaffer's script and the underplaying of the performance as resulting in a "perfect cameo." Calling Jessica Tandy's performance "excellent," Atkinson describes her portrait of the mother as "a trifle too anxiously well-bred, overwrought in the best of taste, sparingly acid, hypocritically cheerful.

*****

S55 **The Physicists** (1964)

**Credits**

| | |
|---|---|
| Play by Friedrich Duerrenmatt | |
| Adaptation by James Kirkup | |
| Producers | Allen Hougdon, Inc. and Stevens Productions, Inc. with Robert Whitehead |
| Director | Peter Brook |
| Scenery, Lighting, Costumes | John Bury |
| Production Supervisor | Lloyd Burlingame |
| Production stage manager | Paul A. Foley |

**Cast**

| | |
|---|---|
| Inspector Richard Voss | Roberts Blossom |
| Maria Boll | Doris Rich |
| Blocher | Jack Woods |
| Guhl | Frank Daly |
| Policemen | John Dutra, Drew Eliot |
| Police Doctor | Alex Reed |
| Herbert Georg Beutler (Newton) | Hume Cronyn |
| Mathilde von Zahnd | Jessica Tandy |
| Ernest Heinrich Ernesti (Einstein) | George Voskovec |
| Lina Rose | Frances Heflin |
| Oskar Rose | David Ford |
| Adolf Friedrich | Terry Culkin |
| Wilfried Kaspar | Leland Mayforth |
| Jorg-Lukas | Doug Chapin |
| Johann Wilhelm Mobius | Robert Shaw |
| Monika Steitler | Elizabeth Hubbard |
| Uwe Sievers | Rod Colbin |
| McArthur | John Perkins |
| Murillo | Leonard Parker |

**The Play's History**

The Physicists had its New York premiere on October 13, 1964 at the Martin Beck Theatre.

**Synopsis**

A comedy set in an asylum run by Fraulein von Zahnd where three voluntary patients, each of them physicists, are feigning insanity. Mobius ("King Solomon") has entered the asylum so that his formula unifying all scientific knowledge may be kept from a world that is morally unprepared to receive it. Beutler ("Newton") and Ernesti ("Einstein") are agents of rival powers who have trailed Mobius to the asylum. They hope to persuade him to join their side. Believing their positions in the asylum to be threatened, the physicists murder their nurses, whereupon the remaining attendants are replaced with bodyguards.

Now the three inmates reveal their real motives to one another. Mobius convinces his two pursuers that to protect humankind they all must remain secluded forever. Their serenity is destroyed when Von Zahnd discloses that she, under the influence of the historical King Solomon, has copied Mobius' documents and placed them at the disposal of a power seeking world domination. Realizing that they are held captive by a truly insane person, the physicists resign themselves to playing out their assumed roles of Solomon, Newton, and Einstein.

**Commentary**

Die Physiker was written in 1962 by Swiss playwright Friedrich Duerrenmatt.

**Reviews**

New York Times (10-14-64)--The Times reviewer sees Duerrenmatt's play as a grimly sardonic and cautionary tale that explores a single thought: how to control the unlimited nuclear powers of destruction that scientists have put at humankind's disposal. Despite director Peter Brook's often external theatrical business, the playwright sums up in compelling allegorical terms for the reviewer the overwhelming problem of our time. Reviewer Howard Taubman describes Jessica Tandy's portrayal of the hunchbacked spinster Fraulein Docktor as having the "required unlovely coldness."

*****

**S56** A Delicate Balance (1966)

**Credits**

Play by Edward Albee

| | |
|---|---|
| Producers | Theatre 1967 (Richard Barr, Clinton Wilder) |
| Director | Alan Schneider |
| Scene Designer | William Ritman |
| Costume Designer | Theoni V. Aldredge |
| Lighting Designer | Tharon Musser |

**Cast**

| | |
|---|---|
| Agnes | Jessica Tandy |
| Tobias | Hume Cronyn |
| Claire | Rosemary Murphy |
| Harry | Henderson Forsythe |
| Edna | Carmen Mathews |
| Julia | Marian Seldes |

**The Play's History**

A Delicate Balance opened on September 12, 1966 at the Martin Beck Theatre.

**Synopsis**

Agnes maintains the delicate balance within her family in Albee's play: her indecisive husband, Tobias; her reformed alcoholic sister Claire who drinks heavily; her daughter Julia who has arrived at her parents' home after her fourth failed marriage. Agnes and Tobias' upper-class suburban lives are unabalanced by the arrival of Harry and Edna, their best friends, who have been seized by an unknown terror. Unable to stay at home, they ask for shelter with their friends. With the house in an uproar, Tobias urges Agnes to decide what to do: should Harry and Edna stay on? Agnes points out that Tobias has always charted the direction of their lives and that she has only maintained his set course. Their dilemma is clear: if Harry and Edna stay, so will the chaotic situation remain; but if they are asked to leave, the friendship will have been proved a meaningless illusion. Then, too, Tobias' relationship with Agnes will be brought into question.

Tobias confronts this dilemma by telling his guests that they are unwelcome but at the same time demanding that they stay. Harry and Edna see through his ploy and return home to face their terrors alone. Agnes comforts Tobias by reassuring him that he did try. With the morning comes order, truthfulness, and hope.

**Commentary**

Like Albee's earlier play, Who's Afraid of Virginia Woolf?, A Delicate Balance touched the same issues, probing the illusory nature of relationships. Albee received the Pulitzer Prize for A Delicate Balance.

**Reviews**

New York Times (9-23-1966)--The line from the play, "That is a condition. I asked about an action," is to the Times reviewer the summation of the Albee play's success and weakness. To write about the hollowness of human lives, Albee has his characters talk and talk but showing, according to the reviewer, might have been preferable. Walter Kerr praises Jessica Tandy as the "silver-haired queen of all that is absent" along with Hume Cronyn's description of his desperately loving encounter with a cat. Reviewer Walter Kerr says that Tandy's finest moment comes in a fierce assault on "human withdrawal, on the evasive action each of us takes when he hears too much pain in the immediate neighborhood." Despite fine performances, Kerr finds Albee's play drained of flesh and suspense.

*****

S57 **Home** (1970)

**Credits**

Play by David Storey

| | |
|---|---|
| Producer | Alexander H. Cohen |
| Director | Lindsay Anderson |
| Designer | Jocelyn Herbert |
| Lighting Designer | Jules Fisher |
| Music | Alan Price |
| Associate Producer | Clinton Wilder |
| Production Associates | Hildy Parks, Roy A. Somlyo |
| Production Supervisor | Jerry Adler |

**Cast**

| | |
|---|---|
| Harry | John Gielgud |
| Jack | Ralph Richardson |
| Marjorie | Dandy Nichols |
| Kathleen | Mona Washbourne |
| Alfred | Graham Weston |

**The Play's History**

Home was first presented on June 17, 1970, by the English Stage Company at the Royal Court Theatre, London. It opened on November 17, 1970 at the Morosco Theatre with its original British cast. During the New York run, Dandy Nichols became ill and Jessica Tandy replaced her in January of 1971.

**Synopsis**

Two middle-aged, respectable men (Gielgud and Richardson) meet in a garden and talk idly through the afternoon. One says he is a heating engineer and the other has manufactured jam. It seems as though they are on holiday and staying in the same hotel. They talk about the past, reminisce about relatives, and relate events of small importance. As they talk, the emptiness and loneliness of their lives are revealed.

Two women (Washbourne and Nichols) enter and talk and flirt with the men. They are louder, more common, and poorer than their male friends. It is soon revealed that they are all mental patients living in an institutional "home."

The play is the story of one day in the lives of these four people in which nothing very much happens. The two men dream and remember happier times that they never experienced. The two women, perhaps more deeply disturbed, chatter like bitchy friends and finally glare coldly at a hostile world. Nevertheless, their relative reasonableness is contrasted by the appearance of a young boy who has had a lobotomy and fancies himself a great wrestler.

**Commentary**

David Storey's play reminded critics of Samuel Beckett's Waiting for Godot in its depiction with four characters of a situation in which people are living out empty lives. Comparisons were also made to Harold Pinter's earlier plays in which characters, speaking colloquially, try to bridge a communications gap.

**Reviews**

New York Times (11-18-70)--The Times reviewer called the acting and staging of Home as "near perfection." Clive Barnes found that John Gielgud and Ralph Richardson were giving two of the greatest performances of their careers in the Storey play.

New York Post (11-18-70)--The Post reviewer again cited the two distinguished British knights, Gielgud and Richardson, for sheer perfection in acting.

*****

**S58** **All Over** (1971)

**Credits**

| | |
|---|---|
| Play by Edward Albee | |
| Producer | Theatre 1971 (Richard Barr, Charles Woodward, Edward Albee) |
| Director | John Gielgud |
| Scenery & Costumes | Rouben Ter-Arutunian |
| Lighting Designer | Richard Nelson |
| Production Stage Manager | Bruce A. Hoover |

**Cast**

| | |
|---|---|
| Wife | Jessica Tandy |
| Daughter | Madeleine Sherwood |
| Mistress | Colleen Dewhurst |
| Doctor | Neil Fitzgerald |
| Son | James Ray |
| Best Friend | George Voskovec |
| Nurse | Betty Field |
| Newspapermen | John Gerstad, Charles Kindl, Allen Williams |

**The Play's History**

All Over opened March 27, 1971 at the Martin Beck Theatre.

**Synopsis**

In All Over, the audience waits in the anteroom during a man's dying along with his doctor, family, and friends. The play is built of a series of operatic arias--musings on death. Though we never see the dying man and learn very little about him except that he is enormously famous, we are aware of the physical fact of his dying. He may be a lawyer, diplomat, statesman, business tycoon. The fact that he dies is the first level of Albee's play. The play's superstructure is the *effect* that the man's death and the fact of death have on the people presumably nearest to him. There develops a sympathy of loss between the man's wife and his mistress. The children are unremarkable offsprings of remarkable parents. The friend, correct to a fault, offers to marry the widow who at one time was his lover.

**Commentary**

All Over is written at that middle moment in playwright Edward Albee's life where he first glimpses those intimations of mortality that includes his own death. The result is an "obituary play."

**Reviews**

New York Times (3-29-71)--Times reviewer, Clive Barnes, calls All Over a "lovely, poignant and deeply felt play" about a man's dying surrounded by an intimate group--doctor, wife, mistress, children, and best friend. Barnes summarizes the play as a mature treatment of that quite final maturity--death without transfiguration. As wife and mistress, Jessica Tandy and Colleen Dewhurst give "lovely performances, one of silver and one of bronze."

*****

**S59** **Noel Coward in Two Keys** (1974)

**Credits**

Plays by Noel Coward

| | |
|---|---|
| Producers | Richard Barr, Charles Woodward |
| Director | Vivian Matalon |
| Setting & Lighting Design | William Ritman |
| Costume Design | Ray Diffen |
| Hair Styles | Ray Iagnocco |
| Production Stage Manager | Mark Wright |
| Associate Producers | Michael Kasdan, Michael Frazier |

**Cast** for **Come into the Garden, Maud**

| | |
|---|---|
| Anna-Mary Conklin | Jessica Tandy |
| Felix | Thom Christopher |
| Verner Conklin | Hume Cronyn |
| Maud Caragnani | Anne Baxter |

**Cast** for **A Song at Twilight**

| | |
|---|---|
| Hilda Latymer | Jessica Tandy |
| Felix | Thom Christopher |
| Hugh Latymer | Hume Cronyn |
| Carlotta Gray | Anne Baxter |

**The Play's History**

Under the title Noel Coward in Two Keys, the two short plays Come into the Garden, Maude and A Song at Twilight opened on February 28, 1974 at the Ethel Barrymore Theatre and ran for 140 performances followed by a national tour.

It was first performed as Suite in Three Keys on London's West End in 1966 starring Sir Noel Coward.

**Synopsis**

The curtain-raiser, Come into the Garden, Maud, depicts a rich American couple vacationing in Switzerland. The woman (Tandy) is a self-made snob and her husband (Cronyn) is a self-made golfer whose bluntness is forever ruining his wife's dinner parties. Circumstances contrive to have the husband (he would have been the 13th at table) sequestered upstairs in their hotel suite when a poor, but beautiful Italian aristocrat (Baxter) comes to say goodby. She is about to leave for Rome in her Volkswagen. The good-natured, bewildered husband and the woman of the world become emotionally entangled, leaving the wife to her just deserts.

In A Song at Twilight, a distinguished English writer waits for a visit from a former mistress. His health is poor and he is guarded by her stolid German wife, a former secretary. The former mistress who was once an actress arrives. She is writing her memoirs and has love letters from the writer that she wants to include in her book. She also has letters that the author wrote to his male secretary.

The request to publish the letters reveals not just the writer's homosexuality but the social conventions that have prevented him for a lifetime from writing from the heart.

**Commentary**

In 1966, Noel Coward conceived the idea of two evenings in repertory in London's West End. One evening was to be a full-length play; the other, a brace of one-act plays. Produced under the generic title, Suite in Two Keys, all three plays took place in the same Swiss hotel suite and starred the author. The major London success was the full-length play, A Song at Twilight. Coward's illness curtailed the London run and subsequent plans to bring both evenings of theatre to Broadway.

Almost a decade later, a double bill arrived on Broadway with the most successful of the plays. The intermission was eliminated from A Song at Twilight and it was packaged with the shorter play, Come into the Garden, Maud. Hume Cronyn was cast in the roles that Noel Coward had written for himself. Legend has it that the irascible homosexual author depicted in A Song at Twilight was modeled on W. Somerset Maugham.

**Reviews**

New York Times (2-25-74)--Clive Barnes called A Song at Twilight "matchless." Hume Cronyn in Coward's role, written for himself, "dances through the performance of his life" and Tandy and Baxter are "faultless" as the two women in his life.

New York Times (3-1-74)--Reviewing for the Times, Mel Gussow focuses on Tandy and Cronyn's 40 years together as an acting team and describes their work together in the Coward play as "ever in tune."

*****

**S60** The Gin Game (1977)

**Credits**

| | |
|---|---|
| Play by D. L. Coburn | |
| Producers | The Shubert Organization |
| Director | Mike Nichols |
| Scene Design | David Mitchell |
| Costume Design | Bill Walker |
| Lighting Design | Ronald Wallace |
| Production Supervisor | Nina Seeley |

**Cast**

| | |
|---|---|
| Fonsia Dorsey | Jessica Tandy |
| Weller Martin | Hume Cronyn |

**The Play's History**

The Gin Game opened on October 6, 1977 at the John Golden Theatre.

**Synopsis**

The Gin Game is set in a dilapidated old people's home which serves as backdrop to the series of card games (gin rummy games) played by the two elderly inmates that reveals their shipwrecked lives, pride, love and anger. Trapped in the spiritual and physical impoverishment that has marked their lives for a lifetime, the two characters continually reach out to each other and slash each other whenever they connect.

As the play opens, Weller is a veteran of the old-age home. A mirror of institutional neglect, he is on the porch playing solitaire because he is a cantankerous rebel. He has disassociated himself from the other inmates (unseen) who watch television, discuss their ailments, and sing hymns. He is playing solitaire, though he would rather be playing gin rummy with a partner.

Fonsia, a new arrival, enters. She is still in shock at finding herself institutionalized. The masterful Weller persuades her to join him at the card table. They play hand after hand. Somehow, Fonsia keeps winning, but she is melancholy and apologetic in victory; he is bluff and hearty in defeat. After a time, this begins to change as Fonsia torments her partner by trying to lose and finally plays with savage triumph.

As they play, they talk and reveal each other's loneliness and poverty and the weaknesses that have left them so alone and poor. His rage at losing mirrors the self-destructive impulse that has wrecked his life. Her ability to win while disguising her will to win, her quiet needling, reflects the sour egoism which has alienated her husband and child.

As the games proceed and become more deadly, the characters alternate between their need for each other and their rejection of each other. In the second scene, Fonsia has revived, combed her hair, put on lipstick, and changed her dress. She has suddenly and temporarily, as it turns out, turned toward life. As the characters' frustrations build up, Weller and Fonsia become living demonstrations of how life kills itself as they again shipwreck themselves in this place for dying.

**Commentary**

D. L. Coburn's play (and first play on Broadway) was first developed at Actor's Theatre of Louisville.

**Reviews**

New York Times (10-7-77)--The Times reviewer celebrates the mesmerizing performances of Jessica Tandy and Hume Cronyn and the seamless direction of Mike Nichols. In praise of the two performers, reviewer Richard Eder describes Tandy as "all unfocused misery at first. She becomes steadily clearer, more self-possessed, more formidable." Each time she says "gin" there is a progression from simple pleasure to sinister pleasure to shouted hatred. She can express 12 different emotions by saying "gin" 12 times. In contrast, Cronyn, according to Eder, finds 12 different ways to calibrate defeat: the tightened mouth, the laugh without mirth, the clenched teeth, etc.

*****

**S61** **Rose** (1981)

**Credits**

| | |
|---|---|
| Play by Andrew Davies | |
| Producers | Elizabeth I. McCann, Nelle Nugent and the Shubert Organization with Colin Brough for the Lupton Theatre Company Ltd. and Warner Theater Productions |
| Director | Alan Dossor |

| | |
|---|---|
| Scene Designer | John Gunter |
| Costume Designer | Linda Fisher |
| Lighting Designer | Andy Phillips |

**Cast**

| | |
|---|---|
| Rose | Glenda Jackson |
| Mother | Jessica Tandy |
| Smale | Beverly May |
| Malpass | Margaret Hilton |
| Jim Beam | J. T. Walsh |
| Sally | Jo Henderson |
| Jake | Guy Boyd |
| Geoffrey | John Cunningham |
| School Caretaker and Teachers | Don McAllen Lesilie, Cynthia Crumlish, Lori Carcilie |

**The Play's History**

Rose opened at the Cort Theatre on March 26, 1981.

**Synopsis**

Rose is the story of a Midlands school teacher in the midst of several midlife crises. She questions the lack of fulfillment in her job teaching six year-old children, in her "dead marriage," and in her relationship with her mother. In an effort to reconnect with her mother during which her mother rejects her once again, Rose makes the first of her many pronouncements to the audience: "This isn't about her," she explains. "This is about me!"

Rose is the play's narrator and addresses the audience as if they were students. Though she is portrayed as indecisive, her marriage is painlessly jettisoned. Her career also seems assured. Her mildly progressive classroom methods entrance a school-system supervisor who invites her to bed. And her feminist views seem mildly mainstream.

The play is made up of direct addresses and comic set-pieces that describe a local flasher, the tedium of school assemblies, and the flirtation between Rose and her extramarital suitor.

**Commentary**

The play was brought to New York as an acting vehicle for Glenda Jackson.

**Reviews**

New York Times (3-27-81)--The Times reviewer was entranced by Jessica Tandy in the supporting role of Rose's mother. Tandy made two appearances at the beginning of each act and reviewer Frank Rich cautioned audiences not to arrive late for either. As the mother of a Midlands schoolteacher,

Tandy's first scene with her daughter in a wine bar creates a "rigid figure in the most sensible clothes simply refusing to have any fun." Though delighted to see Glenda Jackson on the New York stage again, Eder found her a "Jean Brodie of teachers, not a shrinking rose."

## S62 Foxfire (1982)

**Credits**

| | |
|---|---|
| Play by Susan Cooper and | Hume Cronyn |
| Producers | Robert Lussier, Warner Theatre Productions Inc., Claire Nichtern, Mary Lea Johnson, Sam Crothers |
| Director | David Trainer |
| Musical Score | Jonathan Holtzman |
| Scene Designer | David Mitchell |
| Costume Designer | Linda Fisher |
| Lighting Designer | Ken Billington |
| Sound Designer | Louis Shapiro |
| Production Stage Manager | Martha Knight |

**Cast**

| | |
|---|---|
| Annie Nations | Jessica Tandy |
| Hector Nations | Hume Cronyn |
| Prince Carpenter | Trey Wilson |
| Holly Burrell | Katherine Cortez |
| Dillard Nations | Keith Carradine |
| Doctor | James Greene |

**The Play's History**

Foxfire, an original play by Hume Cronyn and Susan Cooper, was developed from the popular folklore anthology and first performed at The Guthrie Theater in Minneapolis. It opened on November 11, 1982 at the Ethel Barrymore Theatre and ran for 213 performances.

**Synopsis**

Set in the Appalachian mountains of Rabun County, Georgia, this stage play of the folklore anthology takes as its central action the fate of the 79 year-old widow, Annie Nations. Descending on her small log-cabin home are a real estate entrepreneur wanting to buy her property for a development site and her prodigal son, a successful "folk" singer, who has apparently sold out to show business interests. He wants to convince his mother to leave her isolated Blue Ridge mountain homestead and live with him and her grandchildren in Florida where he has marital problems. Hector Nations, now dead five years, is the play's narrator and the story of the Nations family is told in flashbacks. The conflict between tradition and progress is embodied in the figure of Annie Nations. The dramatic question of the play is, "Should she turn her back on the land that her husband worked his whole life and his father before him and where she has lived out a lifetime? This question and its painful resolution are the interest of the play.

**Commentary**

Inspired by the popular folklore anthologies, Foxfire was developed over several seasons at the Stratford Festival Theatre (Canada) and The Guthrie Theater (Minneapolis) with Jessica Tandy as the central figure, Annie Nations. While critics decried the failure of the play to establish the fiery Tandy-Cronyn interplay as in their past vehicles, audiences were stunned by the single moment when Tandy was asked to jump back 62 years in a flashback to the time Annie Nations was first courted by her husband. The actress leaped high into the air in a lithe, controlled movement and with a few jig steps transformed an aged woman into a dewy girl.

**Reviews**

New York Times (11-12-82)--Writing for the Times, Frank Rich pronounced that Jessica Tandy was the only real reason to see Foxfire. "Everything this actress does is so pure and right that only poets, not theatre critics, should be allowed to write about her." He described her legendary performance as the 79 year-old Appalachian matriarch, Annie Nations, as "brilliant," exceptionally so in her Act II transformation from an aged woman into a young girl. Critical of the patchwork writing and the predictable performances of the remaining cast, Rich lamented the failure of the play to provide substantial scenes between Tandy and Cronyn.

*****

**S63** **The Glass Menagerie** (1983)

**Credits**

Play by Tennessee Williams

| | |
|---|---|
| Producers | Elizabeth I. McCann, Nelle Nugent, Maurice Rosenfield, Lois F. Rosenfield, Ray Larsen |
| Director | John Dexter |
| Scenic Designer | Ming Cho Lee |
| Costume Designer | Patricia Zipprodt |
| Lighting Designer | Andy Phillips |

| | |
|---|---|
| Music | Paul Bowles |
| Sound | Otts Munderloh |

**Cast**

| | |
|---|---|
| Amanda Wingfield | Jessica Tandy |
| Tom Wingfield | Bruce Davidson |
| Laura Wingfield | Amanda Plummer |
| The Gentleman Caller | John Heard |

**The Play's History**

This Broadway revival of Tennessee Williams' The Glass Menagerie opened on December 1, 1983 at the Eugene O'Neill Theatre. Written in 1944 and originally titled The Gentleman Caller, The Glass Menagerie opened in Chicago in 1945 with Laurette Taylor in the role of Amanda Wingfield and with Eddie Dowling as Tom. The production moved to Broadway the following year and was voted the best play of the year by the New York Drama Critics Circle.

**Synopsis**

The Glass Menagerie is a "memory" play narrated by Tom Wingfield who exists both without and within the play. He is a merchant seaman who within seven scenes narrates his memories of his closing days in a St. Louis tenement with his mother and sister. The father was a telephone man who long ago "fell in love with long distances." The family survives with Tom, the poet, working in a warehouse during the day and going to movies at night. His sister Laura, crippled from a childhood illness, is unable to cope with adulthood and retreats into the fantasy world of her glass animal collection from which the play takes its title. Their mother Amanda sells magazine subscriptions in support of the family while clinging to her youthful illusions of a more gentle life in the Mississippi Delta and the exhilaration of receiving seventeen gentlemen callers in one afternoon.

The story of the characters' needs and desperate courage is told in seven scenes. Amanda dreams of marrying the shy Laura to a suitable young man. This dream is shattered when Tom brings a "gentleman caller" to dinner at his mother's insistence. The outsider introduces hope, companionship, and sympathy into Laura's life only to announce that he is engaged to be married. When he departs, Amanda keeps up the pretense that Laura will have other suitors, but Laura and Tom can no longer share their mother's illusions about the life she imagines is just around the corner for them: success and marriage. Laura retreats into the safe, imaginary world of her glass menagerie and Tom escapes, like his father before him, to freedom although not from his guilt for abandoning his sister and mother.

**Commentary**

In 1945, The Glass Menagerie marked Tennessee Williams first major success and established him as an important playwright. Two years later with the resounding Broadway success of A Streetcar Named Desire, Williams was acclaimed as the "new" Eugene O'Neill.

Like O'Neill's Long Day's Journey into Night, The Glass Menagerie is an autobiographical play that transforms the Williams family of St. Louis into the Wingfield family. The narrator, who bears the author's own name Tom, leads the audience through a series of scenes in family life dominated by his doting, manipulative mother, Amanda, the quintessential Southern belle.

**Reviews**

New York Times (12-2-83)--The Times reviewer expressed nostalgia for the reunion of Tennessee Williams and Jessica Tandy for the first time in a generation following A Streetcar Named Desire. While the revival left much to be desired in the staging and supporting cast, according to Frank Rich, the performance of Jessica Tandy was not to be missed. It is Tandy's ability to give us "truth in the pleasant disguise of illusion that makes her performance a piece of music that lingers in our minds as persistently as Amanda lingered in the author's."

*****

**S64** **The Petition** (1986)

**Credits**

Play by Brian Clark

| | |
|---|---|
| Producer | Robert Whitehead, Roger L. Stevens and the Shubert Organization with Astramead Ltd. and Freeshooter Productions Ltd. |
| Executive Producer | Nathan Joseph |
| Director | Peter Hall |
| Production Designer | John Bury |

**Cast**

| | |
|---|---|
| Lady Elisabeth Milne | Jessica Tandy |
| Gen. Sir Edmund Milne | Hume Cronyn |

**The Play's History**

The Petition opened on April 24, 1986 at the John Golden Theatre. It brought together a new play by British playwright Brian Clark, author of Whose Life Is it Anyway?, and the production team of Sir Peter Hall and John Bury.

It also brought together the acting team of Tandy and Cronyn for a final time in their long stage careers.

**Synopsis**

A petition has been signed by Lady Elisabeth Milne in violation of the rules of her Tory class and the narrow convictions of her husband, a retired general, Sir Edmund Milne. She has also joined a public protest against nuclear armaments. What proceeds is a legalistic debate on the lessons that society learned both from England's glory days of colonial Empire and from Chamberlain's appeasement of Hitler. Their inconclusive ideological arguments are upstaged by several surprise revelations about the Milnes' long marital history. Like political history, the Milnes' marriage is seen as an unwinnable war whose skirmishes are papered over, if not resolved, by a constantly amended truce.

The plot's centerpiece is Elisabeth's explanation as to why she was driven to take a stand against war so late in life. She tells the old soldier before her: "You always said it's the last battle that counts."

**Commentary**

Tandy and Cronyn's performances in The Petition were viewed as a valedictory to their illustrious stage careers. As the elderly woman told her elderly husband an unbearably sad secret, the audience sat in the presence not of the Milnes of Belgravia but of the play's stars, an acting phenomenon now unique in the Broadway theatre and possibly never to come its way again.

In a New York Times feature article published five days before the opening, Tandy and Cronyn announced that The Petition would be their last stage performance in a two-character play, explaining the rigors of a "two-hander" as too great for actors in their late seventies.

**Reviews**

New York Times (4-25-86)--Dismissing Brian Clark's play as a "high-minded television sketch," reviewer Frank Rich proceeded to celebrate the legendary theatrical relationship of Jessica Tandy and Hume Cronyn as one of the most illustrious marriages in the history of the American stage. "The script accomplishes its essential job," Rich wrote, "which is to show off Mr. Cronyn and Miss Tandy to as much comic and touching effect as the circumstances of age will allow."

## Beyond Broadway
## 1949-1985

**S65** Now I Lay Me Down to Sleep. Memorial Auditorium, Stanford University, CA. July 22, 1949. Tandy was one of six professional actors who performed with Stanford University drama students in Elaine Ryan's play directed by Hume Cronyn.

**S66** The Little Blue Light. Brattle Theatre, Cambridge, MA. August 14, 1950. Hume Cronyn acted and directed Edmund Wilson's play with Tandy in the cast.

**S67** Madam, Will You Walk. Phoenix Theatre, New York. December 1, 1953. A comedy by Sidney Howard; co-directed by Hume Cronyn and Norman Lloyd.
Cast: Jessica Tandy, Hume Cronyn, Norman Lloyd, Robert Emmett, Susan Steell, Leon Janney. (Closed January 10, 1954) New York Times (12-20-53) said: Madam, Will You Walk is a "funny comedy with iconoclastic attitudes toward life" in which Jessica Tandy after A Streetcar Named Desire and The Fourposter is having "an actor's holiday."

**S68** The Fourposter. City Center, New York. January 5, 1955. Tandy and Cronyn played the popular revival at City Center.

**S69** A Day By the Sea. ANTA Theatre, New York. September 26, 1955. A play by N. C. Hunter; directed by Cedric Hardwicke.
Cast: Jessica Tandy, Hume Cronyn, Aline MacMahon, Halliwell Hobbes, Dennis King, Veronica Cole, Barclay Hodges, Leo Britt, Megs Jenkins, John W. Austin. New York Times (9-27-55) said: A Day by the Sea is pleasantly written, shrewdly directed, and brilliantly acted.

**S70** Triple Play. Playhouse, New York. April 15, 1959. Tandy appeared in this triple bill of one-acts as Miss Lucretia Collins in Portrait of a Madonna by Tennessee Williams, as Angela Nightingale in Bedtime Story and as the Innocent Bystander in Pound on Demand by Sean O'Casey. The plays were directed by Hume Cronyn.

**S71** Five Finger Exercise. National Touring Company; 1960-61.

**S72-73** Macbeth, Troilus and Cressida. The American Shakespeare Festival Theatre, Stratford, Connecticut. June-July 1961. Macbeth (June 6, 1961) by William

Shakespeare; directed by Jack Landau; with scenery, costumes and lighting by Robert O'Hearn, Motley, and Tharon Musser.
Cast: Donald Davis, James Ray, Ted van Griethuysen, Pat Hingle, Donald Harron, Richard Waring, Paul Sparer, Patrick Hines, William Larsen, Alan Marlowe, Bill Fletcher, Will Geer, Hiram Sherman, Billy Partello, Jessica Tandy, Carrie Nye, Kim Hunter, Carla Huston, Kathryn Loder. New York Times (6-19-61)--Jessica Tandy is singled out for her praiseworthy portrait of "undaunted mettle" as Lady Macbeth. Her Lady Macbeth was described by Howard Taubman as "a study in leashed ambition and rage" whose evil is conveyed by the tight, icy hardness of her speech. Not so fortunate was Pat Hingle's Macbeth who had not yet "mastered the ease of vocal production" demanded by the role.

Troilus and Cressida (July 23, 1961) by William Shakespeare; directed by Jack Landau; with scenery, costumes, and lighting by Robert O'Hearn, Motley, and Charles Elson.
Cast: Pat Hingle, Ted van Griethuysen, Jessica Tandy, Kim Hunter, Carrie Nye, Hiram Sherman, Patrick Hines, Alek Primrose, Donald Davis, Donald Harron. New York Times (7-24-61)--This Troilus and Cressida, transposed to the "romantic period" of the American Civil War, was not a successful setting for Shakespeare's fierce and bitter anti-war play, according to reviewer Howard Taubman. "The production verges on puerility," he wrote. However, Donald Davis as Achilles, Paul Sparer as Ulysses, Jessica Tandy as Cassandra, Kim Hunter as Helen, and Pat Hingle as Hector gave "effective" performances.

**S74** Big Fish, Little Fish. Duke of York's Theatre, London. September 18, 1962. Tandy played Edith Maitland opposite Hume Cronyn.

**S75-77** Hamlet, The Three Sisters, Death of a Salesman. The Guthrie Theater, Minneapolis. May-July 1963. In the first season of Tyrone Guthrie's Minnesota Theatre Company Jessica Tandy played Gertrude in Shakespeare's Hamlet, Olga in Chekhov's The Three Sisters, and Linda Loman in Arthur Miller's Death of a Salesman at the Guthrie Theater.

Hamlet (May 7, 1963) by William Shakespeare; directed by Tyrone Guthrie; designed by Tanya Moiseiwitsch.
Cast: Graham Brown, Paul Ballantyne, Ken Ruta, Lee Richardson, Jessica Tandy, Nicolas Coster, Robert Pastene, George Grizzard, Ellen Geer, Alfred Rossi, Michael Levin, John Cromwell, Ruth Nelson, Clayton Corzatte, Claude Woolman, Ed Preble, Ken Ruta. New York Times (5-9-63)--The reviewer, celebrating the opening of the new theatre and the birth of the Minnesota Theatre Company, praises the theatricalism of Guthrie's modern-dress staging and the performances of George Grizzard as Hamlet, Lee Richardson

as Claudius, and Jessica Tandy as a "gentle and confused" Gertrude.

The Three Sisters (June 18, 1965) by Anton Chekhov; directed by Tyrone Guthrie; designed by Tanya Moiseiwitsch.
Cast: Jessica Tandy, Rita Gam, Ellen Geer, Ruth Nelson, Zoe Caldwell, Robert Pastene, Hume Cronyn, George Grizzard, Lee Richardson, Claude Woolman, Charles Cioffi, Ed Preble, Clayton Corzatte. New York Times (6-20-63)--The Times review called the production remarkably well balanced and marked by solid ensemble playing.

Death of a Salesman (July 16, 1963) by Arthur Miller; directed by Douglas Campbell; with scenery and costumes by Randy Echols and Carolyn Parker.
Cast: Hume Cronyn, Jessica Tandy, Nicholas Coster, Lee Richardson, Ken Ruta, Helen Backlin, Paul Ballantyne, John Cromwell, Alfred Rossi, Janet MacLachlan, Michael Levin, Judith Doty, Joan Van Ark, Carol Emshoff, John Lewin. New York Times (7-20-63)--Praising the company's ability to play classical and modern texts, the Times reviewer cited the play's relevance for our affluent society and the notable performances of Hume Cronyn as a "cocky and distracted" Willy Loman and Jessica Tandy as his patient and understanding wife.

**S78-80** The Way of the World, The Cherry Orchard, The Caucasian Chalk Circle. The Guthrie Theater, Minneapolis. May-August 1965.

A revival of The Way of the World (May 11, 1965) by William Congreve; directed by Douglas Campbell; production designed by Tanya Moiseiwitsch.
Cast: Ann Whiteside, Robert Milli, Robert Pastene, Ken Ruta, Paul Ballantyne, Ed Flanders, Graham Brown, Jessica Tandy, Zoe Caldwell, Nancy Wickwire, Ellen Geer, Helen Harrelson, Krinstina Callahan, Evie McElroy, Niki Flacks, Earl Boen, James Lineberger, James J. Lawless, Ann Whiteside, John Cappalletti, Donald West, Bruce Allard, Edouard Blitz, Dave Karr. New York Times (6-2-65)--The Times reviewed the Minnesota Theatre Company's production as uneven in its playing but had high-praise for Zoe Caldwell ("unfaltering in every velvet thrust") as Millamant, Jessica Tandy as Lady Wishfort, Nancy Wickwire as Marwood, and Robert Pastene as Fainall.

A revival of The Cherry Orchard (June 15, 1965) by Anton Chekhov; directed by Tyrone Guthrie; production designed by Tanya Moiseiwitsch.
Cast: Jessica Tandy, Kristina Callahan, Nancy Wickwire, Robert Pastene, Lee Richardson, Ken Ruta, Paul Ballantyne, Ruth Nelson, Hume Cronyn, Ellen Geer, Sandy McCallum, Ed Flanders, Alvah Stanley. New York Times (8-2-65)--The Times reviewer contrasted productions of Chekhov's play performed at the Guthrie Theater and at Canada's Stratford Festival Theatre. Tyrone Guthrie's staging was considered more intrusive than John Hirsch's at Stratford but reviewer Howard Taubman found both performances by Kate Reid and

Jessica Tandy as Ranevskaya not full portraits of Chekhov's impulsive and generous central figures.

A revival of The Caucasian Chalk Circle (August 3, 1965) by Bertolt Brecht; Tandy played a "peasant" in the Prologue in this production with Zoe Caldwell as Grusha.

**S81** A Delicate Balance. National Touring Company. 1967. Tandy played Agnes in the national tour of Albee's play.

**S82** The Miser. Mark Taper Forum, Los Angeles. 1968. Tandy played Frosine opposite Hume Cronyn's Harpagon in the Center Theatre Group production of Moliere's play.

**S83** Heartbreak House. The Shaw Festival, Niagara-on-the-Lake, Ontario, Canada. July 5, 1968. Revival of the play by George Bernard Shaw; directed by Val Gielgud with scenery and costumes by Maurice Strike and Hilary Corbett.
Cast: Eleanor Beecroft, Diana Leblanc, Tony Van Bridge, Frances Hyland, Jessica Tandy, Patrick Boxill, Paxton Whitehead, Bill Fraser, James Valentine, Kenneth Wickes.
New York Times (7-6-68)--With unequivocal praise for the festival's artistic director, Paxton Whitehead, and for the cast of Heartbreak House, Times reviewer, Dan Sullivan, calls the production one "worth going to London to see." Especially praiseworthy, according to the reviewer, were the performances of Jessica Tandy as Hesione Hushabye and Tony Van Bridge as Captain Shotover in this most difficult of Shavian plays.

**S84** Tchin-Tchin. Ivanhoe Theatre, Chicago. 1969. Tandy played Pamela Pew-Pickett.

**S85** Camino Real. Lincoln Center Repertory Company, Vivian Beaumont Theatre, New York. January 8, 1970. Revival of the play by Tennessee Williams; directed by Milton Katselas; sceney and costumes by Peter Wexler; lighting by John Gleason.
Cast: Patrick McVey, Michael Enserro, Victor Buono, Jose Perez, Leta Bonynge, Jean-Pierre Aumont, Ralph Drischell, Barbara eda-Young, Arthur Sellers, Luis Avalos, Michael Levin, Joan Pringle, Joseph Mascolo, Sam Umani, Michael Miller, Priscilla Pointer, Antonia Rey, Jose Barrera, Roberta Reyes, Sylvia Syms, Susan Tyrell, Arnold Soboloff, Al Pacino, Paul Benjamin, Robert Keesler, Robert Sumonds, Ralph Bell, Philip Bosco, Nick Cantrell, Jessica Tandy, Clifford David, Michael Levin, Dan Sullivan. New York Times (1-9-70) called Camino Real a lovely play of genuinely poetic vision. As Camille, Jessica Tandy is

marvelous as "she walks in the ashes of a great beauty with all the dignity of an exiled queen."

**S86** Promenade All. National Touring Company. 1972-73.

**S87** Happy Days. Forum Theatre, Repertory Theatre Company at Lincoln Center, New York. November 20, 1972. Play by Samuel Beckett; directed by Alan Schneider with scenery and lighting by Douglas W. Schmidt and John Gleason; costumes by Sara Brook.
Cast: Jessica Tandy and Hume Cronyn as Winnie and Willie. New York Times (11-21-72)--Decrying the soon-to-be demise of the Forum Theatre, reviewer Clive Barnes found the Beckett festival production of Happy Days (and Act Without Words I) with its cheeky despair and perky illusions appropriate for the theatre's closing. Barnes compared Jessica Tandy's Winnie with earlier renderings by Madeleine Renaud, Brenda Bruce, and Ruth White. Of Tandy, Barnes wrote of her "special shrill-voiced gentility" in the role. "Her performance seems lean with the frustrations of memory," he wrote, "a memory struggling with the present yet sparsely immediate with the essence."

**S88** Not I. Forum Theatre, Repertory Theatre of Lincoln Center, New York. November 22, 1972. Play by Samuel Beckett; directed by Alan Schneider with scenery and lighting by Douglas W. Schmidt and John Gleason.
Cast: Jessica Tandy. New York Times (11-23-76)--Reviewing a world premiere of Beckett's Not I (played on a double-bill with Krapp's Last Tape), Clive Barnes described the event as a "brief and puzzling, squalid night-time cry against the monstrous regiment of death." The Mouth in Not I was beautifully played by Jessica Tandy. Barnes wrote: "It is almost an abstract sense of fear and desolation that Miss Tandy's torrential voice and her spot-lighted, carefully enunciating lips seem to suggest."

**S89** Happy Days and Not I. National Touring Company. 1973.

**S90** Noel Coward in Two Keys. National Touring Company. 1975.

**S91-93** The Way of the World, A Midsummer Night's Dream, Eve. Stratford Shakespeare Festival Theatre, Ontario, Canada. June 1976. The 23rd season of Canada's Stratford Festival opened with The Way of the World on June 7, 1976 at the Festival Stage. Play by William Congreve;

directed by Robin Phillips with scenery and lighting by Daphne Dare and Gil Wechsler.
Cast: Alan Scarfe, Jeremy Brett, Frances Fagan, Stuart Hutchison, Gregory Wanless, Keith Batten, Keith Baxter, Bernard Hopkins, Mia Anderson, Domini Blythe, Maggie Smith, Jackie Burroughs, Jan Kudelka, Larry Lamb, Jessica Tandy, Barbara Stephen, Peter Hutt, Cathy Wallace. New York Times (6-6-76)--With praise for artistic director Robin Phillips' transformation of the Stratford company into one of the three leading companies in the English-speaking theatre (Britain's National Theatre and Royal Shakespeare Company are the other two named), reviewer Clive Barnes delights in the key relationship between Congreve's Millamant and Mirabell as played by Maggie Smith and Jeremy Brett. Among the gallery of Congreve dupes were Jessica Tandy as a frantic Lady Wishfort valiantly fighting off old age "as if it were the plague."

**S94** Long Day's Journey into Night. Theatre London, Ontario, Canada. 1977. Tandy played Mary Tyrone in the production directed by Robin Phillips.

**S95** The Gin Game. National Touring Company. U.S. cities, Canada, and U.S.S.R. 1978-79.

**S96** The Gin Game. Lyric Theatre, London. July 21, 1979.

**S97-98** Foxfire, Long Day's Journey into Night. Stratford Shakespeare Festival Theatre, Ontario, Canada. 1980. Tandy played Annie Nations in the play by Susan Cooper and Hume Cronyn, and Mary Tyrone in the play by Eugene O'Neill.

**S99** Foxfire. The Guthrie Theater, Minneapolis. 1982. Tandy played Annie Nations again in the play's pre-Broadway production directed by Marshall W. Mason.

**S100** Salonika. New York Shakespeare Festival Public Theatre, New York. April 2, 1985. Tandy played Charlotte in Louise Page's play directed by John Madden with Elizabeth Wilson, David Strathairn, Thomas Hill, and Maxwell Caulfield. Scenery, costumes, and lighting by Andrew Jackness, Dunya Ramicova, and Paul Gallo. As an octogenarian English widow visiting the Greek island with her spinsterish daughter Tandy was called "always superbly expressive as the quirky and crochety old lady" amused by a widower's attentions (Variety 4-24-85).

**S101** <u>Foxfire</u>. Ahmanson Theatre, Los Angeles. 1985. Tandy performed in the revival with Hume Cronyn directed by David Trainer.

Karl Malden and Jessica Tandy as Mitch and Blanche DuBois in *A Streetcar Named Desire* (1947). (This and the following photographs are courtesy of the Billy Rose Theatre Collection, The New York Public Library for the Performing Arts, Astor, Lenox and Tilden Foundations.)

Jessica Tandy and Hume Cronyn in *The Fourposter* (1951).

Jessica Tandy as Louise Harrington in *Five Finger Exercise* (1959).

Jessica Tandy and Hume Cronyn as Agnes and Tobias in *A Delicate Balance* (1966).

Jessica Tandy as Fonsia Dorsey in *The Gin Game* (1977).

Jessica Tandy and Glenda Jackson in *Rose* (1981).

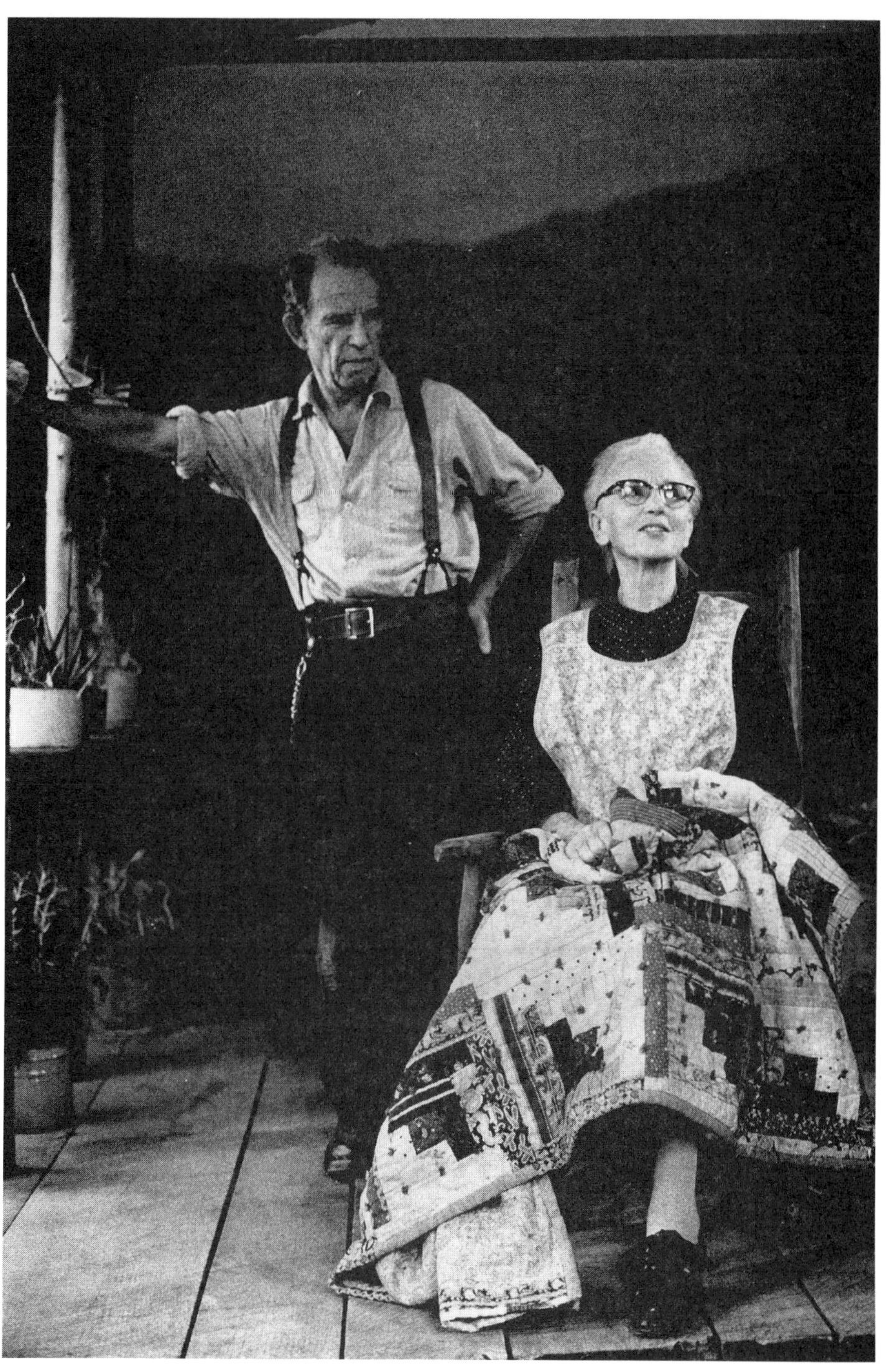

Hume Cronyn and Jessica Tandy as Hector and Annie Nations in *Foxfire* (1982).

# Filmography

**F01** **THE INDISCRETIONS OF EVE**
(British International Pictures; 1932; 63 minutes)

**Credits**

| | |
|---|---|
| Director/Producer/Screenplay | Cecil Lewis |
| Camera | James Wilson, Philip Grindrod |
| Music | Marius B. Winter and Orchestra |

**Cast**

| | |
|---|---|
| Eve | Steffi Duna |
| Sir Peter Martin | Fred Conyngham |
| Ralph | Lester Matthews |
| Pip | Tony Sympson |
| Maid | Jessica Tandy |
| Butler | Clifford Heatherley |
| Simms | Hal Gordon |
| Mother | Muriel Aked |
| Father | Arthur Chesney |
| Smart | George Mozart |
| Barman | Teddy Brown |

**Synopsis**

The love affair between a wealthy aristocrat and a poor English shop girl is the subject of this musical comedy. Steffi Duna is the girl who earns her living in a dressmaker's shop. She has reproduced her own features on a mannequin in the window. Conyngham investigates the likeness and Duna's charms captivate him. He pursues her until she agrees to marry him.

**Commentary**

This is a simple-minded rich-boy-meets-poor-girl story but notable since Jessica Tandy makes her first film appearance in a walk-on as the Maid.

**Reviews**

The Times (London) (5-23-32)--The Times reviewer labeled the film "good farcical entertainment."

*****

**F02** **MURDER IN THE FAMILY**
(20th Century Fox; 1938; 75 minutes)

**Credits**

Based on the novel by James Ronald

| | |
|---|---|
| Director/Producer | Albert Parker |
| Screenplay | David Evans |

**Cast**

| | |
|---|---|
| Stephen Osborne | Barry Jones |
| Ann Osborne | Jessica Tandy |
| Dorothy Osborne | Evelyn Ankers |
| Ted Fleming | Donald Gray |
| Edith Osborne | Jessie Winter |
| Michael Osborne | David Markham |
| Marjorie Osborne | Glynis Johns |
| Peter Osborne | Roddy McDowall |
| Aunt Octavia | Annie Esmond |
| Miss Mimms | Rani Wallie |

Also: Claire Arnold, A. Bromley Davenport, Stella Arbenina, W. Simpson Fraser, David Arnold, Edgar K. Bruce, Charles Childerstone.

**Synopsis**

In this murder mystery, Barry Jones as Stephen Osborne is accused of killing his wealthy Aunt Octavia after she refuses to help him out of a financial bind. The real culprit is the disaffected maid who stabs her mistress upon learning that she has been included in the inheritance.

**Commentary**

The ponderous material makes the actors' hard work a waste. Jessica Tandy plays the long-suffering wife of the accused in her second film.

*****

**F03** **THE SEVENTH CROSS**
(MGM; 1944; 111 minutes)

**Credits**

Based on the novel by Anna Seghers

| | |
|---|---|
| Director | Fred Zinnermann |
| Producer | Pandro S. Berman |
| Screenplay | Helen Deutsch |
| Camera | Karl Freund |
| Musical Score | Roy Webb |
| Editor | Thomas Richards |
| Art Director | Cedric Gibbons, Leonid Vasian |
| Set Decoration | Edwin B. Willis, Mac Alper |
| Costumes | Irene |
| Special Effects | A. Arnold Gillespie, Danny Hall |
| Makeup | Jack Dawn |

**Cast**

| | |
|---|---|
| George Heisler | Spencer Tracy |
| Toni | Signe Hasso |
| Paul Roeder | Hume Cronyn |
| Liesel Roeder | Jessica Tandy |
| Mme. Marelli | Agnes Moorehead |
| Franz Marnet | Herbert Rudley |
| Poldi Schlamm | Felix Bressart |
| Wallau | Ray Collins |
| Zillich | Alexander Granach |
| Mrs. Sauer | Katherine Locke |
| Bruno Sauer | George Macready |
| Fiedler | Paul Guilfoyle |
| Dr. Lowenstein | Steven Geray |
| Leo Herman | Kurt Katch |
| Leni | Karen Verne |
| Fuellgrabe | Konstantin Shayne |
| Bellani | George Suzanne |
| Overkamp | John Wengraf |
| Fahrenberg | George Zucco |
| Hellwig | Steven Muller |
| Fraulein Bachmann | Eily Malyon |

Also: Fay Wall, William Challee.

**Synopsis**

In the three years preceding the start of World War II, seven prisoners escape from a Nazi concentration camp. The commandant places crosses on seven trees for the prisoners to be nailed to and left to die when they are recaptured. One by one the escapees are recaptured and only one cross remains, the one intended for Spencer Tracy.

Embittered by his years of captivity, Tracy as George Heisler has lost all faith in humankind. He narrowly escapes capture by the Gestapo time and time again as he makes his way to safety in neutral Holland. Various friends and strangers, including the Roeders (Jessica Tandy and Hume Cronyn), help him along the way. He reaches safety with his faith in humanity restored and as a different man from the hollow shell that survived the death camp.

**Commentary**

Spencer Tracy's performance was brilliant and many of the small parts were beautifully acted, especially Hume Cronyn as an old friend who assists Tracy and Jessica Tandy who plays Cronyn's wife. This was Tandy's first Hollywood film; she would continue to be cast in minor, undistinguished roles until she left Hollywood and returned to the stage. This was also the first film in which Tandy and Cronyn played husband and wife which they were in real life. They would play many such roles in films and on stage throughout their long careers.

When released in 1944, The Seventh Cross was criticized for taking too sympathetic a view of the German people as victims themselves of a criminal regime. However, the film stands as one of the best anti-Nazi films that Hollywood produced during the war years.

**Reviews**

New York Times (10-5-44)--The Times reviewer expressed reservations about a film that was sympathetic toward the German people. Despite objections to its subject, the reviewer praised the film's suspenseful escape story and the splendid performances, especially those of Spencer Tracy as the hunted man, Hume Cronyn as the friend that helps him, and Jessica Tandy as Cronyn's courageous wife.

Variety (7-19-44)--The trade paper hailed Anna Seghers' novel and Helen Deutsch's screenplay as a suspenseful tale of Nazi bestiality and human endurance. Pointing out that Mrs. Seghers was herself a refugee from the Third Reich, the Variety reviewer was fairly objective about the humanizing of the German people who assisted Spencer Tracy in his arduous escape from the Nazis.

*****

**F04 THE VALLEY OF DECISION**
(MGM; 1945; 118 minutes)

**Credits**

Based on the novel by Marcia Davenport

| | |
|---|---|
| Director | Tay Garnett |
| Producer | Edwin H. Knopf |
| Screenplay | John Meehan, Sonya Levien |
| Camera | Joseph Ruttenberg |
| Musical Score | Herbert Stothart |

| | |
|---|---|
| Editor | Blanche Sewell |
| Art Direction | Cedric Gibbons, Paul Groesse |
| Set Decoration | Edwin B. Willis, Mildred Griffiths |
| Special Effects | A. Arnold Gillespie, Warren Newcombe |

**Cast**

| | |
|---|---|
| Paul Scott | Gregory Peck |
| Mary Rafferty | Greer Garson |
| William Scott | Donald Crisp |
| Pat Rafferty | Lionel Barrymore |
| Jim Brennan | Preston Foster |
| Constance Scott | Marsha Hunt |
| Clarissa Scott | Gladys Cooper |
| McCready | Reginald Owen |
| William Scott, Jr. | Dan Duryea |
| Louise Kane | Jessica Tandy |
| Delia | Barbara Everest |
| Ted Scott | Marshall Thompson |
| Julia Gaylord | Mary Lord |
| Giles, Earl of Moulton | John Warburton |
| Mrs. Gaylord | Mary Currier |
| Callahan | Arthur Shields |
| Mr. Laurence Gaylord | Russell Hicks |
| Callahan | Arthur Shields |
| Kate Shannon | Geraldine Wall |
| Mrs. Callahan | Evelyn Dickson |
| Paulie | Dean Stockwell |
| Stella | Joy Harrington |
| Dr. McClintock | Lumsden Hare |

Also: Norman Ollstead, Connie Gilchrist, Pearl Curtis, William O'Leary, Richard Abbott, Anna Q. Nillson, Sherlee Collier, Mike Ryan.

**Synopsis**

A poor-girl-meets-rich boy story set against a background of the steel industry in Pittsburgh in 1870. Greer Garson, a young Irish woman, takes a position as a domestic in the imposing home of Donald Crisp as William Scott, a steel magnate. Garson's father, Lionel Barrymore, is a former steel worker who has been permanently handicapped in an accident in a mill owned by Crisp. At issue are the mill's safety practices. Barrymore opposes his daughter's new job with the "enemy."

Once on the Crisp estate, Garson becomes invaluable to the family--to Crisp's wife and four children. Gregory Peck, one of Crisp's son, and Garson fall in love but she believes they cannot marry because of the differences in their social status. Even the father, who adores Garson, agrees to the marriage but the couple's happiness is shortlived. A strike takes place at the mill backed by Garson's father and the marriage is postponed. Crisp calls in professional strikebreakers and Garson herself tries to mediate by arranging a face-to-face meeting between her father and Crisp. They arrive for the meeting with their supporters and a fight breaks out. In the turmoil, Barrymore and Crisp are killed and Garson feels responsible. She leaves her job and Peck and spends the next decade a lonely woman.

Meanwhile, Peck has married Jessica Tandy, a shrewish individual. He is unhappy in the marriage but does nothing to extricate himself. His mother suffers a heart attack and asks for Garson but Tandy resists Garson's return fearing that her husband will leave her. Gladys Cooper, as Clarissa Scott, dies, and now the steel mill is owned by the Crisp children and by Garson who has inherited a share from the late Mrs. Crisp. Two of the Crisp sons want to sell the mill but Peck, Garson, and Marsha Hunt vote to keep the mill.

By this time, Tandy thoroughly hates Garson and verbally abuses her. At the film's end, it is uncertain that Peck will leave Tandy for Garson but there is the suggestion that they will find happiness even in unconsummated love.

**Commentary**

The film, based on Marcia Davenport's popular novel, was a huge success, earning $6 million in its initial release. Greer Garson received her fifth Best Actress "Oscar" nomination. Once again, Jessica Tandy and Hume Cronyn were cast together in this film but the diminutive Cronyn was replaced when it became obvious that he would never be credible as the brother of the lanky Gregory Peck.

In the unsympathic role of the shrewish wife, Tandy is cited by critics as one of the film's villains along with Lionel Barrymore and Dan Duryea.

**Reviews**

New York Times (5-4-45)--Critical of the film's failure to portray Marcia Davenport's monumental novel, the reviewer concentrated on the Cinderella story in which Greer Garson enters a Pittsburgh steel baron's home as a domestic and emerges as beloved by the family and nobly influencing its traditions. Garson was called "more photogenic than incisive."

Variety (4-11-45)--The trade paper pronounced The Valley of Decision as a certain box office success under Tay Garnett's skillful direction.

*****

**F05** **THE GREEN YEARS**
(MGM; 1946; 127 minutes)

**Credits**

| | |
|---|---|
| Based on the novel by | A. J. Cronin |
| Director | Victor Saville |
| Producer | Leon Gordon |
| Screenplay | Robert Ardrey, Sonya Levien |
| Camera | George Folsey |
| Musical Score | Herbert Stothart |
| Editor | Robert J. Kern |
| Art Direction | Cedric Gibbons, Hans Peter |
| Special Effects | A. Arnold Gillespie, Donald Jahraus |

**Cast**

| | |
|---|---|
| Alexander Gow | Charles Coburn |
| Robert Shannon | Tom Drake |
| Alison Keith | Beverly Tyler |
| Papa Leckie | Hume Cronyn |
| Grandma Leckie | Gladys Cooper |
| Robert Shannon (as child) | Dean Stockwell |
| Mama Leckie | Selena Royle |
| Kate Leckie | Jessica Tandy |
| Jason Reid | Richard Haydn |
| Saddler Boag | Andy Clyde |
| Adam Leckie | Norman Lloyd |
| Murdoch Leckie | Robert North |
| Jamie Nigg | Wallace Ford |
| Alison Keith (as child) | Eilene Janssen |
| Gavin Blair | Hank Daniels |
| Gavin Blair (as child) | Richard Lyon |
| Canon Roche | Henry O'Neill |
| Blakely | Henry Stephenson |
| Mrs. Bosomley | Norma Varden |

**Synopsis**

This faithful filmization of A. J. Cronin's novel traces a young boy's growth to manhood in Scotland. Charles Coburn as Alexander Gow is the young boy's great-grandfather who is fond of the local brew and is forever in trouble despite his endearing qualities. Dean Stockwell as the younger Robert Shannon is a fascinated observer of Coburn's misdemeanors. Tom Drake plays the boy at an older age as he experiences the joys of attending school and falling in love. What the boy wants most is to go to college which is achieved, unhappily, through insurance money inherited after his beloved great-grandfather's death.

**Commentary**

The Green Years is a faithful and convincing filmization of A. J. Cronin's popular novel about a boy's growing up.

Jessica Tandy and Hume Cronyn continue to be cast in the same film. Cronyn plays the mean-spirited head of the household that takes the boy in and Tandy plays his daughter, Kate Leckie, one of the many undistinguished ingenue roles that she played in Hollywood in the 1940s.

**Reviews**

New York Times (4-4-46)--The basic foundation of the film, the Times reviewer asserted, was the tender relationship between the boy and the Micawberish relative. Charles Coburn as the swag-bellied old rascal gave a memorable performance.

Variety (3-13-46)--The Variety reviewer praised the film-makers' skill at transforming a best-selling novel into a popular movie. Victor Saville's direction was praised for its restrained and subtle ability to translate mood and characterization to the screen.

*****

**F06 DRAGONWYCK**
(20th Century Fox; 1946; 103 minutes)

**Credits**

Based on the novel by Anya Seton

| | |
|---|---|
| Director/Screenplay | Joseph L. Mankiewicz |
| Producer | Darryl F. Zanuck |
| Camera | Arthur Miller |
| Musical Score | Alfred Newman |
| Editor | Dorothy Spencer |
| Art Direction | Lyle Wheeler, J. Russell Spencer |
| Set Decoration | Paul S. Fox |
| Costume | Rene Hubert |
| Special Effects | Fred Sersen |
| Choreography | Arthur Appel |

**Cast**

| | |
|---|---|
| Miranda Wells | Gene Tierney |
| Ephraim Wells | Walter Huston |
| Abigail Wells | Ann Revere |
| Nicholas Van Ryn | Vincent Price |
| Dr. Jeff Turner | Glenn Langan |
| Madga | Spring Byington |
| Katrina Van Ryn | Connie Marshall |
| Bleecker | Henry Morgan |
| Johanna Van Ryn | Vivienne Osborne |
| Peggy O'Malley | Jessica Tandy |
| Elizabeth Van Borden | Trudy Marshall |
| Count De Grenier | Reinhold Schunzel |
| Tabitha | Jane Nigh |
| Cornelia Van Borden | Ruth Ford |

| | |
|---|---|
| Obadiah | David Ballard |
| Tom Wells | Scott Elliott |
| Tompkins | Boyd Irwin |
| Countess De Grenier | Maya Van Horn |
| Mr. MacNabb | Keith Hitchcock |
| Doctor | Francis Pierlot |

Also: Arthur Thompson, Al Winter, Larry Steers, Wallace Dean, Tom Martin, Edwin Davis, Selby Bacon, Ruth Cherrington, Elizabeth Williams, John Chollot, Virginia Lindley, Nanette Vallon, George Ford, Alexander Sacha, Nestor Eristoff, Ted Jordan, William Carter, Mickey Roth Jamie Dana, Robert Walter Baldwin, Harry Humphrey, Robert Malcolm, Trevor Bardette, Arthur Ayleworth, Tom Fadden, Clancy Cooper, Addison Richards, Betty Fairfax, Douglas Wood, Steve Olsen, Gertrude Astor, Charles Waldron, Grady Sutton.

**Synopsis**

In this Gothic murder story which takes place in the 1840s, Vincent Price is a Dutch landowner living on a large estate in New York's Hudson valley. He exploits the tenant farmers and resents his wife because she has been unable to bear him a son, only a daughter. Gene Tierney, a distant relative, arrives to act as the daughter's governess. Price falls in love with her and, unknown to her, poisons his wife. He then marries Tierney and she gives birth to a son but the infant dies. At this point, Price becomes even more psychologically unbalanced and begins using drugs.

The local doctor, played by Glenn Langan, discovers that Price murdered his first wife just as he plans to eliminate Tierney.

**Commentary**

Gothic murder and madness are featured in this intelligent adaptation of Anya Seton's popular novel. Vincent Price was sensational in the role of the deranged husband; his success type-cast him for many years. Dragonwyck was Joseph L. Mankiewicz's first directorial job and the effort established him as a force in the film business.

Jessica Tandy again has a minor, undistinguished role as Peggy O'Malley. With her fourth film it is becoming apparent that Hollywood casting directors do not know either how to cast her or how to utilize her considerable talents.

**Reviews**

New York Times (4-11-46)--The Times reviewer called the film an obvious repetition of the Bluebeard story with all its elemental features including a forbidden tower, the arrogant husband as killer, and an atmosphere of terror. Dismissing Gene Tierney as ornamental, the reviewer praised

Vincent Price's performance as formidable in its "suave diabolism."

Variety (2-20-46)--The trade paper praised the film as a compelling transition from Anya Seton's book to the screen. Vincent Price was cited as playing one of his best roles to date as a brooding pathological case.

*****

**F07** **FOREVER AMBER**
(20th Century Fox; 1947; 140 minutes)

**Credits**
Based on the novel by Kathleen Winsor

| | |
|---|---|
| Director | Otto Preminger |
| Producer | William Perlberg |
| Screenplay | Philip Dunne, Ring Lardner, Jr., Jerome Cady |
| Camera (Technicolor) | Leon Shamroy |
| Musical Score | David Raksin |
| Music Direction | Alfred Newman |
| Editor | Louis Loeffler |
| Art Direction | Lyle Wheeler |
| Set Decoration | Thomas Little, Walter M. Scott |
| Costumes | Charles LeMaire, Rene Hubert |
| Special Effects | Fred Sersen |
| Fights | Fred Cavens |

**Cast**

| | |
|---|---|
| Amber St. Clair | Linda Darnell |
| Bruce Carlton | Cornel Wilde |
| Lord Almsbury | Richard Greene |
| King Charles II | George Sanders |
| Captain Rex Morgan | Glenn Langan |
| Earl of Radcliffe | Richard Haydn |
| Nan Britton | Jessica Tandy |
| Mother Red Cap | Ann Revere |
| Black Jack Mallard | John Russell |
| Corinna Carlton | Jane Ball |
| Sir Thomas Dudley | Robert Coote |
| Matt Goodgroome | Leo G. Carroll |
| Countess of Castlemaine | Natalie Draper |
| Mrs. Song | Margaret Wycherly |
| Lady Redmond | Alma Kruger |
| Lord Redmond | Edmond Breon |
| Landale | Alan Napier |
| Little Bruce | Perry "Bill" Ward |
| Bob Starling | Richard Bailey |
| Mrs. Starling | Houseley Stevenson |

Also: Bob Adler, Gilchrist Stuart, David Murray, Arthur Elliott, Skelton Knaggs, Peter Shaw, Jimmy Ames, Vernon

Downing, Lillian Moliere, Ian Keith, Frederic Worlock, Norma Varden, Edith Evanson, Ellen Corby, James Craven, Tempe Pigott, Cyril Delevanti, Cecil Weston, Ottola Nesmith, Pati Behrs, Eric Noonan, Robert Greig, Glenn Langan, Tim Huntley, Jimmy Lagano, Tom Stevenson, Boyd Irwin, Leonard Carey, Will Stanton, C. C. "Tex" Gilmore, David Ralston, Victoria Horne.

**Synopsis**

Linda Darnell has the featured role as the beautiful seventeenth-century English girl born into poverty who discovers promiscuity as the path to wealth and happiness. She takes several lovers (Wilde, Russell, and Langan) and eventually becomes the favorite concubine of King Charles II (George Sanders). Nevertheless, promiscuity has its price and Darnell loses the only man she has ever loved, Cornell Wilde, who leaves her and takes their child to America.

**Commentary**

Based on the racy novel by Kathleen Winsor and a lavish production ($4 million dollars), the film of Forever Amber suffers from its inability to detail the eroticism that was the novel's distinction and appeal due to the censorship problems encountered in Hollywood in the 1940s. The novel was an instant bestseller and sold three million copies.

Cast as Nan Britton, Jessica Tandy plays Linda Darnell's maid.

**Reviews**

New York Times (10-23-47)--Restricted by the Hollywood Production Code, the reviewer found the film story of Amber St. Clare greatly reduced in numbers of marriages, lovers, and children. In this lavish production, the Times reviewer described Linda Darnell's performance as without subtlety.

Variety (10-15-47)--The reviewer called the film a surefire box office success as a spectacular story of the rise and fall of a king's mistress with its wealth of seventeenth-century knavery and debauchery.

*****

**F08** **A WOMAN'S VENGEANCE**
(Universal; 1947; 95 minutes)

**Credits**

Based on the short story, "The Gioconda Smile" by Aldous Huxley

| | |
|---|---|
| Director and Producer | Zoltan Korda |
| Screenplay | Aldous Huxley |
| Camera | Russell Metty |
| Musical Score | Miklos Roza |
| Editor | Jack Wheeler |
| Art Direction | Bernard Herzbrun, Eugene Lourio |
| Set Decoration | Russell A. Gausman, T. F. Offenbecker |
| Costumes | Orry-Kelly |

**Cast**

| | |
|---|---|
| Henry Maurier | Charles Boyer |
| Doris Maurier | Ann Blyth |
| Janet Spence | Jessica Tandy |
| Dr. Libbard | Sir Cedric Hardwicke |
| Nurse Braddock | Mildred Natwick |
| Gen. Spence | Cecil Humphreys |
| Emily Maurier | Rachel Kempson |
| Robert Lester | Hugh French |
| Clara | Valerie Cardew |
| Coroner | Carl Harbord |
| Prosecuting Counsel | John Williams |
| First Warder | Leyland Hodgson |
| Maisey | Ola Lorraine |
| McNabb | Harry Cording |
| Bit | Frederick Worlock |

**Synopsis**

Charles Boyer as Henry Maurier is accused of murdering his invalid wife, Rachel Kempson, because of an affair he had with a younger woman, Ann Blyth, whom he married soon after his wife's death. All evidence points to his guilt until the real killer, Jessica Tandy, makes a last-minute confession and saves Boyer from execution. Portrayed as a love-starved spinster whose passion is unrequited, Tandy murdered Boyer's first wife to get revenge for his failure to return her affection. The neurotic nurse, Mildred Natwick, is used as Tandy's tool for vengeance. The film's highpoint is the last-minute struggle of minds between the family doctor, Sir Cedric Hardwicke, and Tandy as the condemned husband awaits his execution.

**Commentary**

A Woman's Vengeance is one of a handful of screenplays that Aldous Huxley, author of the Brave New World, wrote for Hollywood. Jessica Tandy and Sir Cedric Hardwicke were singled out for their stellar performances and the scene in which Hardwicke wrings from Tandy the last-minute confession by turning the hands of the clock forward one hour was the highpoint of the film.

**Reviews**

New York Times (2-4-48)--Dismissing the film as an easily predictable affair, the Times reviewer, nevertheless, praised Jessica Tandy and Sir Cedric Hardwicke for their critical performances in Huxley's treatise on vengeance. In the final scene of revelation, Tandy gave a "brilliant show of vicious determination" matched only by Hardwicke's resoluteness.

Variety (12-24-47)--Praising the film's performances, Variety cited in particular Jessica Tandy as the love-starved spinster in a "standout performance." The reviewer conceded that the film was a highly polished, talky melodrama saved by a "top caliber" cast.

*****

**F09 SEPTEMBER AFFAIR**
(Paramount; 1950; 91 minutes; Video: Paramount)

**Credits**

Based on a story by Fritz Rotter

| | |
|---|---|
| Director | William Dieterle |
| Producer | Hal B. Wallis |
| Screenplay | Robert Thoeren |
| Camera | Charles B. Lang, Victor Milner |
| Musical Score | Victor Young |
| Editor | Warren Low |
| Art Direction | Hans Dreier, Franz Bachelin |
| "September Song" | Kurt Weill and Maxwell Anderson (sung by Walter Huston) |

**Cast**

| | |
|---|---|
| Manina Stuart | Joan Fontaine |
| David Lawrence | Joseph Cotton |
| Maria Salvatini | Francoise Rosay |
| Catherine Lawrence | Jessica Tandy |
| David Lawrence, Jr. | Robert Arthur |
| Johnny Wilson | Jimmy Lydon |
| Grazzi | Fortunio Bonanova |
| Bianca | Grazia Narciso |
| Rosita | Anna Demetrio |
| Vittorio Portini | Lon Steele |
| Mr. Peppino | Frank Yaconelli |
| Charles Morrison | Charles Evans |
| Francisco | Jimmy Frasco |

Also: Charles La Torre, Gilda Oliva, Saverio Lomedico, George Nardelli, Nick Borgani, Jeanne Lafayette, Dino Bolognese, Georgia Clancey, Dick Elliott, Rudy Rama, Iphigenie Castiglione, Inez Palange, Zacharias Yaconelli, Vitor Desny, James R. Scott, Stan Johnson, Douglas Grange, Larry Arnold, Walter Merrill, Christopher Dark.

**Synopsis**

In this simple romance, Joan Fontaine and Joseph Cotton are traveling to New York from Rome. She is a concert pianist scheduled to give a performance and he is returning to his work, to his marriage on the verge of divorce, and to a son he seldom sees. Their airplane develops engine trouble and lands in Naples. They go sightseeing, thereby missing its departure. As they start to make other airline reservations, they find out that their original plane has crashed and they have been reported dead. Sensing they are in love with each other and knowing that they are listed among the plane's dead, they begin a new life together in Italy.

Somewhat later, Cotton's wife, Jessica Tandy, and his son arrive in Italy. She is willing to give him a divorce but both Cotton and Fontaine realize that they cannot ignore responsibility and the past. Both return to New York and their respective lives with memories of a September romance in Italy.

**Commentary**

The film is most memorable for Kurt Weill's nostalgic "September Song" which the late Walter Huston made immortal in Knickerbocker Holiday. The song is the film's thematic inspiration (an autumn affair) and the sound-track leitmotif.

**Reviews**

New York Times (2-2-1951)--The Times reviewer called September Affair a wistful romance with a "hopelessly silly story with a haunting song." Jessica Tandy was described as putting on a "dreary act as the moist-nosed and thin-flanked" wife whom the great American industrialist is prepared to give up.

Variety (9-6-50)--The trade paper reviewed the film as a clever combination of culture and commercialism. The point was made that the film's story did not require great dramatic acting; however, Jessica Tandy and Robert Arthur, as wife and son, were cited for their strong performances.

*****

**F10 THE DESERT FOX**
(20th Century Fox; 1951; 88 minutes;
Video: CBS/Fox)

**Credits**

Based on the biography by Desmond Young
Director Henry Hathaway
Producer/Screenplay Nunnally Johnson

| | |
|---|---|
| Camera | Norbert Brodine |
| Musical Score | Daniele Amfitheatrof |
| Editor | James B. Clark |
| Art Direction | Lyle Wheeler, Maurice Ransford |
| Set Decoration | Thomas Little, Stuart Reiss |
| Special Effects | Fred Sersen, Ray Kellogg |

**Cast**

| | |
|---|---|
| Erwin Rommel | James Mason |
| Dr. Karl Strolin | Cedric Hardwicke |
| Frau Rommel | Jessica Tandy |
| Hitler | Luther Adler |
| Gen. Burgdof | Everett Sloane |
| Field Marshal Von Rundstedt | Leo G. Carroll |
| Gen. Fritz Bayerlein | George Macready |
| Aldinger | Richard Boone |
| Col. Von Stauffenberg | Eduard Franz |
| Desmond Young | Himself |
| Manfred Rommel | William Regnolds |
| Gen. Schultz | Charles Evans |
| Admiral Ruge | Walter Kingsford |
| Keitel | John Hoyt |
| Gen. Maisel | Don De Leo |
| Rommel's Driver | Richard Elmore |
| Major Walker | John Vosper |
| Commando Captain | Dan O'Herlihy |
| Commando Colonel | Scott Forbes |
| British Medic | Victor Wood |
| British Officer | Lester Matthews |
| Maid | Mary Carroll |
| Col. Von Hofaker | Paul Cavanagh |
| Jodl | Jack Baston |
| German Major | Carleton Young |
| German Surgeon | Freeman Lusk |
| British Medical Officer | Robert Coote |
| Jock | Sean McClory |
| Doctor | Lumsden Haree |
| Stulpnagel | John Goldsworthy |
| German major | Ivan Triesault |
| Desmond Young's Voice | Michael Rennie, Trevor Ward, Philip Van Zandt |

**Synopsis**

The film opens with British commandos making a night attack on the headquarters of General Erwin Rommel in North Africa during World War II. The purpose of the raid is to kill Rommel. Despite slaughter of German troops, Rommel survives. Desmond Young, a Lieutenant-Colonel in the British Army, is taken prisoner and ordered to approach the British battery under a flag of truce to halt its firing on the Germans. Young refuses but before he can be punished the elusive German leader tells his officer that Young is correct. Young recognizes Field Marshal Rommel and then narrates the career of the enigmatic German officer from his North African command to his death by suicide in 1944.

James Mason, as Rommel, is shown commanding his troops just before El Alamein where British soldiers under General Montgomery's command decimated German tanks and armor. His forces in shambles, Mason wires Berlin for permission to withdraw his troops. An order from Hitler instructs Mason to stand firm. George Macready, as Bayerlein, Rommel's best field commander, objects to Hitler's order. Mason disobeys the Fuhrer and orders his troops pulled back. Nevertheless, Mason's order comes too late and the Africa Corps collapses for lack of food, equipment, and petrol.

By this time, Mason is back in Germany recovering from an illness. He is visited by Cedric Hardwicke, a physician and one of a group of conspirators planning to assassinate Hitler to save Germany from utter destruction. He tries to enlist Mason's help but is put off. Mason is next assigned command of the French coastal defenses. Months later, Hardwicke visits Mason once again at his home in Germany where Mason all but agrees to join the conspirators. In an interview with Hitler, Mason discovers how insane the German dictator has become and joins the conspirators.

Mason is wounded during the invasion of Normandy and is sent home to recuperate from his wounds. Meanwhile, Eduard Franz, as Stauffenberg, plants a bomb in Hitler's remote battle headquarters and just misses killing him. The conspirators are systematically rounded up and executed.

Everett Sloane visits Mason and tells him that Berlin knows of his involvement in the conspiracy. He is told that if he demands a public trial his family will be in jeopardy. If he takes the poison that Sloane has brought, then his family will remain safe. Mason dresses in military uniform and leaves with Hitler's emissaries to die as his wife, Jessica Tandy, and son, Regnolds, watch the car drive away.

The film closes with scenes showing Mason commanding troops in the desert, the place of his greatest victories and fame. British Prime Minister Winston Churchill is heard in a voiceover describing Rommel's gallantry as a loyal German soldier who made a gallant effort to rescue Germany from Hitler's leadership.

**Commentary**

This was the first film that attempted to humanize a World War II German military leader--Field Marshal Erwin Rommel. James Mason was magnetic in his portrayal of Rommel who is respected by his Africa Corps as well as by his British and American opponents. Though the film properly belongs to Mason, the supporting cast was excellent and director Henry Hathaway's semi-documentary style brisk. Luther Adler gave an unforgettable cameo performance as Hitler and Jessica Tandy was excellent in a brief appearance as Rommel's wife.

**Reviews**
New York Times (10-18-51; 10-28-51)--The Times reviewer objected to the "strange disregard" in the film for the principles and sensibilities of those who fought Germany and berated the screenwriter and associates for the "deification" of Rommel. James Mason was credited with an outstanding performance as the "misunderstood" type and Jessica Tandy as the "wistful" wife. The second Times review, also written by Bosley Crowther, continued to berate the "soft-hearted" film about the German general. The filmmakers' moral judgment and good taste were questioned.

Variety (10-3-51)--This reviewer also attacked the film for its sympathetic portrait of Erwin Rommel and the "whitewashing" of a number of Hitler's military leaders. To discredit the film, the writer cited the lack of "star" names to lure ticket-buyers but admitted that scenes between James Mason and Jessica Tandy had "sound emotional value."

****

**F11 THE LIGHT IN THE FOREST**
(Walt Disney; 1958; 93 minutes;
Video: Walt Disney)

**Credits**
Based on the novel by Conrad Richter

| | |
|---|---|
| Director | Herschel Daugherty |
| Producer | Walt Disney |
| Screenplay | Lawrence Edward Watkin |
| Camera (Technicolor) | Ellsworth Fredericks |
| Musical Score | Paul J. Smith |
| Editor | Stanley Johnson |
| Music | Franklyn Marks |
| Art Direction | Carroll Clark |
| Set Direction | Emile Kuri, Fred Maclean |
| Costumes | Chuck Keehne, Gertrude Casey |
| Makeup | Pat McNalley |
| Title Song (music/lyrics) | Paul J. Smith and Gil George |
| "I Asked My Love a Favor" | Paul J. Smith and Lawrence E. Watkin |

**Cast**

| | |
|---|---|
| Johnny Butler/True Son | James MacArthur |
| Shenandoe Hastings | Carol Lynley |
| Del Hardy | Fess Parker |
| Wilse Owens | Wendell Corey |
| Milly Elder | Joanne Dru |
| Myra Butler | Jessica Tandy |
| Chief Cuyloga | Joseph Calleia |

| | |
|---|---|
| John Elder | John McIntire |
| Half Arrow | Rafael Campos |
| Harry Butler | Frank Ferguson |
| Niskitoon | Norman Fredric |
| Kate Owens | Marian Seldes |
| Col. Henry Bouquet | Stephen Bekassy |
| George Owens | Sam Buffington |

**Synopsis**

James MacArthur plays a white man raised by Indians in pre-Revolutionary times who is forcibly returned to his people following the signing of a peace treaty between British Colonial Forces and the Delaware Indians. Fess Parker, an Army scout, is assigned to supervise the young man's adjustment. Difficulties arise when MacArthur meets his brutal uncle, Wendell Corey, who takes part in murderous attacks on Indian villages. Carol Lynley is Corey's indentured servant who initially despises MacArther because her parents were killed by marauding Indians. Nevertheless, the two fall in love but Corey kills one of MacArthur's Indian friends and he returns to his tribe only to find that they want to use him as a decoy to ambush innocent people. He refuses and returns to confront Corey whom he beats senseless, having learned that there are good and bad individuals in any situation. MacArthur and Lynley then set off into the wilderness to build a peaceful life together while Parker settles down with the local minister's daughter, Joanne Dru.

**Commentary**

Conrad Richter's novel deals with the theme of the young man at odds with society and is made into a typical Walt Disney adventure film. Well-developed characters and a reasonably intelligent examination of the issues are the film's strong points. The socially-aware Disney films of the fifties were superior to their bland live-action films during the following decade (Mary Poppins is the notable exception).

The Light in the Forest marked Carol Lynley's debut and the start of a long relationship between the studio and James MacArther. It was, however, the end of Fess Parker's work for Disney; he had grown weary of being type-cast as the strong frontiersman. Jessica Tandy as Myra Butler has another unmemorable supporting role.

**Reviews**

New York Times (7-11-58)--The Times reviewer debunked the intellectual content of the film as being a homespun tale on the level of a twelve-year old.

Variety (4-30-58)--The trade paper acknowledged the "wholesome adventure" features of the Disney production along with its salutary lesson in tolerance.

****

**F12** **ADVENTURES OF A YOUNG MAN**
(20th Century Fox; 1962; 145 minutes)

**Credits**

| | |
|---|---|
| Based on stories by Ernest Hemingway | |
| Director | Martin Ritt |
| Producer | Jerry Wald |
| Screenplay | A. E. Hotcher |
| Camera (CinemaScope) | Lee Garmes |
| Musical Score | Franz Waxman |
| Editor | Hugh S. Fowler |
| Art Direction | John Martin Smith, Paul Groesse |
| Set Decoration | Walter M. Scott, Robert Priestly |
| Costumes | Don Feld |

**Cast**

| | |
|---|---|
| Nick Adams | Richard Beymer |
| Carolyn | Diane Baker |
| Contessa | Corinne Calvel |
| Mr. Turner | Fred Clark |
| Billy Campbell | Dan Dailey |
| Telegrapher | James Dunn |
| Bugs | Juano Hernandez |
| Dr. Adams | Arthur Kennedy |
| Major Padula | Ricardo Montalban |
| Rosanna | Susan Strasberg |
| Mrs. Adams | Jessica Tandy |
| John | Eli Wallach |
| Brakeman | Edward Binns |
| Ludstrum | Whit Bissell |
| Montecito | Philip Bournef |
| Ad Francis | Paul Newman |
| Sig Griffi | Tullio Carminati |
| Eddy Bolton | Marc Cavell |
| Major | Charles Fredericks |
| Joe Bolton | Simon Oakland |
| George | Michael J. Pollard |
| Billy Tabeshaw | Pat Hogan |

**Synopsis**

Based upon the early short stories of Ernest Hemingway the film is centered upon his youth as "Nick Adams." Richard Beymer plays the Hemingway surrogate who begins his adventures in rural Michigan. He goes to New York City where he encounters various characters, including Dan Dailey as a drunken advance man for a cooch show for whom Beymer briefly works; Ricardo Montalban as a sympathic Italian officer commanding Beymer in France during World War I; Eli Wallach as a hospital orderly who assists him when he becomes an ambulance officer; Paul Newman as the alcoholic punch-drunk fighter, Ad Francis. Wounded in the war, Beymer falls in love with an ill-starred nurse, Susan Strasberg, who dies at the film's end.

**Commentary**
Early in the film Jessica Tandy plays the Hemingway hero's mother, Mrs. Adams. Hers is one of a number of cameo roles, including Paul Newman's memorable performance as Ad Francis, the decrepit boxer.

**Reviews**
Variety (6-20-62)--The reviewer called the film "a near-miss" largely due to mechanical directing and Beymer's portrayal of the young Hemingway. Praising the number of fine cameo performances, the reviewer described Tandy as "excellent" as the fanatical, domineering mother.

****

**F13 THE BIRDS**
(Universal; 1963; 120 minutes; Video: MCA/Universal)

**Credits**
Based on the story by Daphne du Maurier

| | |
|---|---|
| Director & Producer | Alfred Hitchcock |
| Screenplay | Evan Hunter |
| Camera (Technicolor) | Robert Burks |
| Musical Score | Bernard Herrmann |
| Editor | George Tomasini |
| Production Director | Norman Deming |
| Set Decoration | Robert Boyle, George Milo |
| Costumes | Edith Head |
| Special Effects | Ub Iwerks |
| Bird Trainer | Ray Berwick |

**Cast**

| | |
|---|---|
| Mitch Brenner | Rod Taylor |
| Melanie Daniels | Tippi Hedren |
| Lydia Brenner | Jessica Tandy |
| Annie Hayworth | Suzanne Pleshette |
| Cathy Brenner | Veronica Cartwright |
| Mrs. Bundy | Ethel Griffies |
| Sebastian Sholes | Charles McGraw |
| Mrs. McGruder | Ruth McDevitt |
| Deputy Al Malone | Malcolm Atterbury |
| Helen Carter | Elizabeth Wilson |
| Deke Carter | Conny Chapman |
| Salesman | Joe Mantell |
| Fisherman | Doodles Weaver |

| | |
|---|---|
| Man in the Elevator | Richard Deacon |
| Man in Front of the Pet Shop with White Poodles | Alfred Hitchcock |
| Postal Clerk | John McGovern |
| Woman | Doreen Lang |

**Synopsis**

Alfred Hitchcock's film deals with the anguish and terror created by a murderous attack of thousands of birds on residents of remote Bodega Bay. At the film's start, Rod Taylor meets Tippi Hedren in a San Francisco pet shop. The playgirl follows him to Bodega Bay ostensibly to deliver a pet bird to a friend. She is attacked by a seagull and receives a minor head wound which causes her to stay overnight with teacher Suzanne Pleschette.

Strange things begin to happen in the village. At an outdoor party children are attacked by flocks of birds that begin to gather in vast numbers on rooftops and telephone wires. Jessica Tandy, as Taylor's lonely and possessive mother, finds a farmhouse wrecked, the farmer dead, and his body shredded. School children, including Taylor's young sister, are viciously attacked by swooping, diving birds. Taylor's sister is saved by Hedren who drags her into the safety of a car.

Down in the fishing village, the local folk cannot believe the story that Hedren and Taylor tell them. A local ornithologist discredits the notion that docile birds, by now there are millions of them, would ever turn against human beings. Then birds attack a gas station, causing a man to drop a lighted match into gasoline spilled by an attendant. The place blows up killing the man. Hedren is trapped inside a telephone booth trying to call for help; birds dive suicidially onto the booth but the glass does not give way. Taylor spirits Hedren away from the birds to his home.

En route, Taylor finds Pleshette, his former girl-friend, pecked to death in her front yard; she has died in an effort to protect some of her school children from the killer birds. That night, Taylor frantically boards up the windows. The birds cover the house, pecking away at the heavy wood as they attempt to get inside. Hearing noises upstairs, Hedren goes into the attic and shines a flashlight on an army of waiting birds who attack her. Taylor rescues her and closes the door.

At dawn, the battered family creeps outside and walks quietly through thousands of birds, gets into the car, and drives slowly away.

**Commentary**

Though the film is not vintage Hitchcock, it is technically a marvel with more than 350 special effects. It is without Hitchcock's usual "MacGuffin" (his term for the item or individual sought that causes all of the suspense such as the uranium in _Notorius_ or the diplomat in _Foreign Correspondent_). In _The Birds_, Hitchcock relies on the shock value of nature revenging itself upon humans. The ornithologist in the film explains that the birds might take revenge on human beings for destroying the planet's ecology.

**Reviews**

New York Times (4-1-63)--This is a tongue-in-cheek review of Hitchcock's horror film as a depiction of the classical furies (the birds) descending on the houses of a jealous mother and resentful ex-girlfriend. Admitting that Hitchcock has contrived sufficient shocks and chills, the reviewer praised the performances of Tippi Hedren, Rod Taylor, and Jessica Tandy.

Variety (3-27-63)--The reviewer called The Birds a "parody of Hitchcock by Hitchcock." Indulging in slickly executed, tongue-in-cheek touches, Hitchcock injected shots of sanguinary horror into a featherweight scenario. A romantic plot with Rod Taylor and Tippi Hedren gave way to the evil infestation of birds. Despite reservations, the reviewer considered the release a future moneymaker.

****

**F14 BUTLEY**
(American Film Theatre, British; 1973; 127 minutes)

**Credits**

Based on the play by Simon Gray

| | |
|---|---|
| Director | Harold Pinter |
| Producer | Ely A. Landau |
| Executive Producer | Otto Plaschkes |
| Screenplay | Simon Gray |
| Camera (Eastmancolor) | Gerry Fisher |
| Editor | Malcolm Cooke |
| Art Direction | Carmen Dillon |

**Cast**

| | |
|---|---|
| Ben Butley | Alan Bates |
| Edna Shaft | Jessica Tandy |
| Joey Keyston | Richard O'Callaghan |
| Anne Butley | Susan Engel |
| Reg Nuttall | Michael Byrne |
| Miss Heasman | Georgina Hale |
| Mr. Gardner | Simon Rouse |
| James | John Savident |
| Train Passenger | Oliver Maguire |

Also: Colin Haigh, Darien Angadi, Susan Woodridge, Lindsay Ingram, Patti Love, Belinda Low.

**Synopsis**

The film, like Simon Gray's play, tells the story of a day in the life of Ben Butley, an instructor of English literature at a London university.

During the course of the day, Alan Bates as Butley learns that he is to experience two divorces: his wife, from whom he is separated, is going to divorce him to remarry a mutual friend; his colleague, Joey Keyston, is moving out of their shared office and flat as well. Moreover, his senior colleague Edna Shaft, Jessica Tandy, has completed her work of twenty years on Byron and has also found a publisher for the manuscript. His wife, Susan Engel, comes to his office to tell Bates of her marriage plans. He is in turn bitchy, childish, ill-tempered, insulting, and generally impossible. He doesn't seem to care about the marriage but cannot tolerate rejection.

Tandy drops by Bates's office to inquire about a student who has been missing seminars. He is condescending and claims to know nothing about the student and refuses to mention her book.

Tandy returns a second time and accuses Bates and Keyston of despising her and then rails at the student who, encouraged by Bates, has complained about her teaching to the Department head. While Bates feigns innocence, Keyston tries to reassure her.

Later, there is a quiet scene between Bates and Tandy. She apologizes for her outburst and he congratulates her on the completion of her book. She asks about Bates's work on T. S. Eliot and is told that he has twenty years to go, implying that he will never finish his study. At the film's end, Bates is alone having alienated all of those around him.

**Commentary**

The film, like the play, echoed with allusions to John Osborne's Look Back in Anger and Kingsley Amis's Lord Jim, though Simon Gray was more concerned with the inner man than with social criticism.

Jessica Tandy as Edna Shaft is the embodiment of grace, intelligence, and clear, appealing self-knowledge regarding her work and status. Alan Bates is also as superb in the film as he was in the stage performance. Butley marked Harold Pinter's debut as a film director.

**Reviews**

New York Times (4-9-1974)--The Times reviewer called Alan Bates's performance "superb" as Simon Gray's character who forces others to abandon him. Butley's sparring partners were cited for their performances: Jessica Tandy as "crisp and direct, simmering against her will, stern but not grim"; Richard O'Callaghan and Michael Byrne as the individuals determined to escape Bates's rage.

Variety (1-23-74)--Praising the American Film Festival subscription presentation of Butley, the Variety reviewer singled out for praise Tandy's portrait of a middle-aged schoolteacher who doesn't seem to understand her students.

****

**F15 HONKY TONK FREEWAY**
(Universal; 1981; 107 minutes; Video: HBO/Cannon)

**Credits**

| | |
|---|---|
| Director | John Schlesinger |
| Producer | Don Boyd, Howard W. Koch, Jr. |
| Assistant Director | Benjy Rosenberg |
| Screenplay | Edward Clinton |
| Camera (Technicolor) | John Bailey |
| Musical Score | George Martin, Elmer Bernstein |
| Editor | Jim Clark |
| Art Direction | Edwin O'Donovan |
| Visual Consultant | Fernando Scarfiotti |
| Costumes | Ann Roth |
| Sound | Larry Jost |

**Cast**

| | |
|---|---|
| Duane Hansen | Beau Bridges |
| Sherm | Hume Cronyn |
| Carmen Shelby | Beverly D'Angelo |
| Carol | Jessica Tandy |
| Major Calo | William Devane |
| Eugene | George Dzundza |
| Ericka | Teri Garr |
| Osvaldo | Joe Grifasi |
| Snapper | Howard Hesseman |
| T. J. Tupus | Paul Jabara |
| Sister Mary Clarise | Geraldine Page |
| Betty Boo Radley | Alice Beardsley |
| Claire Calo | Frances Lee McCain |
| Sister Mary Magdalen | Deborah Rush |

Also: Daniel Stern, David Rauche, Sandra McCabe, Kenny Roker, Celia Weston, Jenn Thompson, Peter Billingsley, Ran Frazier, Jerry Hardin, John Ashton, John C. Becher, Davis Roberts, Loretta Tupper, Francis Bay, Rollin Moriyama, Kimiko Hiroshige, James Staley, Shelley Batt, Jason Keller, Shane Keller, Kelly Lange, Kent Williams, Arnold Johnson, Nancy Parsons, Jessica Rains, Ann Risley, Helen Hanft, Don Morgan, Paul Keenan, Robert Stoneman, Randy Norton, Ann Coleman, Gordon Haight, Jack Thibeau, Martha Gehman, George Solomman, Dick Christie, Anita Dangler, Mags Kavanaugh, Gloria Leroy.

**Synopsis**

The film's plot deals with the efforts of a small Florida town, Ticlaw, to have a freeway exit ramp go through their dying community. The mayor, William Devane, bribes some officials to ensure the ramp's construction but is double-crossed and forced to trick motorists into venturing into Ticlaw. Among the hapless travelers who arrive in Ticlaw are: Jessica Tandy and Hume Cronyn, a wacky elderly couple; Beverly D'Angelo, a voluptuous young woman wandering the country in a pink Edsel with the ashes of her dead mother sitting on her car's dashboard; Geraldine Page, a disillusioned nun; two bank robbers, George Dzundza and Joe Grifasi; and Beau Bridges, author of a disastrous children's book entitled _Randy The Carnivorous Pony_.

**Commentary**

The film cost $25 million and grossed only $500,000. Director John Schlesinger (_Midnight Cowboy_ and _The Falcon and the Snowman_) structured the on-the-road comedy by cross-cutting among dozens of characters, creating a movie that only occasionally succeeded.

The scenes with Tandy and Cronyn as a retired advertising man and his alcoholic wife were some of the most successful.

**Reviews**

_New York Times_ (8-21-81)--The _Times_ reviewer found the film "as surprisingly funny as it is silly." This road film had too many equally important characters to keep any one in focus and the reviewer said that Schlesinger needed to be a juggler, not a director. Performances selected for praise were Jessica Tandy and Hume Cronyn as an advertising man and his alcoholic wife who declared proudly that her husband invented bad breath.

_Variety_ (8-18-81)--Less enthusiastic than the _Times_, _Variety_ pronounced the film devoid of basic human appeal. With its thin storyline, large numbers of unsympathetic and undesirable people, and dismal sense of humor, the reviewer predicted the film's commercial failure.

****

**F16 STILL OF THE NIGHT**
(MGM-UA; 1982; 91 minutes; Video: CBS/Fox)

**Credits**

Based on a story by David Newman and Robert Benton

| | |
|---|---|
| Director | Robert Benton |
| Producer | Arlene Donovan |

| | |
|---|---|
| Associate Producers | Kenneth Utt, Wolfgang Gattes |
| Assistant Director | Wolfgang Gattes |
| Screenplay | Robert Benton |
| Camera (Technicolor) | Nestor Almendros |
| Musical Score | John Kander |
| Editor | Jerry Greenberg |
| Production Design | Mel Bourne |
| Art Direction | Michael Molly |
| Set Decoration | Steve Jordan |
| Costume Design | Albert Wolsky |
| Associate Producers | Kenneth Utt, Wolfgang Glattes |
| Assistant Director | Wolfgang Glattes |

**Cast**

| | |
|---|---|
| Sam Rice | Roy Scheider |
| Brooke Reynolds | Meryl Streep |
| Grace Rice | Jessica Tandy |
| Joseph Vitucci | Joe Grifasi |
| Gail Phillips | Sara Botsford |
| George Bynum | Josef Sommer |
| Heather Wilson | Rikke Borge |
| Murray Gordon | Irving Metzman |
| Mugger | Larry Joshua |
| Auctioneer | Tom Norton |
| Mr. Harris | Richmond Hoxie |
| Mr. Chang | Hyon Cho |
| Girl | Danielle Cusson |
| Night Watchman | John Bentley |
| Elevator Operator | George A. Tooks |
| Receptionist | Sigrunn Omark |
| Car Thief | Randy Jurgenson |

Also: Palmer Deane, William Major, Joseph Priestly, Will Rose, Arnold Glimcher, Jeffrey Hoffeld, Linda Le Roy Janklow, Elinor Klein, Susan Patricof.

**Synopsis**

Roy Scheider as a Manhattan psychiatrist finds his own life endangered after one of his patients is murdered. Meryl Streep is the dead man's neurotic, chain-smoking mistress whose distressed, unpredictable behavior leads Scheider to conjecture that she may be the killer.

Streep insinuates herself into Scheider's personal life (he is recently divorced) along with the police who accuse him of withholding evidence on his murdered patient based on the immunity of the doctor-patient relationship. Caught up in his romantic attraction to Streep, Scheider becomes determined to discover if she is the killer. He discusses the case with Jessica Tandy, his mother, who is also a psychiatrist. He plots to entrap Streep and retraces a dream his patient recounted to him and discovers the murderer's identity. In the suspenseful resolution, Scheider and Streep almost lose their lives.

**Commentary**

Still of the Night (originally entitled Stab) is a radical departure for Robert Benton (Kramer vs. Kramer) who was determined to make a suspense film. There are recognizable influences from Alfred Hitchcock's North By Northwest, Psycho, Vertigo, and Saboteur. In his first film after All That Jazz, Roy Scheider is effective as the introspective psychiatrist who finds himself at the center of a homicide investigation.

**Reviews**

Variety (11-3-82)--The film was praised as a literate, well-acted modern suspense thriller influenced by Hitchcock's masterful work. Though cognizant of serious flaws in the plotting, the reviewer gave highmarks to the supporting cast, including Jessicia Tandy as Scheider's psychiatrist-mother, Josef Sommer as the murdered man who appears in flashbacks, and Joe Grifasi as the persistent detective. Streep's performance as a deeply disturbed individual was criticized as failing to provide the pull of sexual mystery that overwhelms Scheider.

*****

**F17 BEST FRIENDS**
(Warner Brothers; 1982; 116 minutes;
Video: Warner)

**Credits**

| | |
|---|---|
| Director | Norman Jewison |
| Producers | Norman Jewison, Patrick Palmer |
| Assistant Director | Win Phelps |
| Screenplay | Valerie Curtin, Barry Levinson |
| Camera (Technicolor) | Jordan Croneweth |
| Musical Score | Michel Legrand |
| Editor | Don Zimmerman |
| Art Direction | Joe Russo |
| Costumes | Betsy Cox |

**Cast**

| | |
|---|---|
| Richard Babson | Burt Reynolds |
| Paula McCullen | Goldie Hawn |
| Eleanor McCullen | Jessica Tandy |
| Tim McCullen | Barnard Hughes |
| Ann Babson | Audra Lindley |
| Tom Babson | Keenan Wynn |
| Larry Weisman | Ron Silver |
| Nellie Ballou | Carol Locatell |
| Lyle Ballou | Noah Hathaway |
| Robbie Ballou | Mikey Martin |
| Jorge Medina | Richard Libertini |
| Carol Brandon | Peggy Walton-Walker |

**Synopsis**

The story follows newlyweds, Burt Reynolds and Goldie Hawn, on a trip to meet their respective families. They are successful Hollywood screenwriters who have upset their cosy domesticity by deciding to marry.

The series of farcical events begins with Reynolds and Hawn holding the ceremony in a Spanish-language wedding chapel in Los Angeles to prevent their friends from finding out they are getting married. They begin their honeymoon in a railway sleeping car where would-be romantic gestures backfire.

Tired and grouchy, they arrive in snowy Buffalo where Hawn's parents, Jessica Tandy and Barnard Hughes, live in intense gloom. Reynolds sleeps alone in Hawn's childhood room still filled with beer mugs from fraternity parties.

In Virginia, Reynolds' family lives in a large condominium complex. His mother, Audra Lindley, takes flash photos of all the moments of her life that she thinks may be "important." Reynolds reverts to eating like his father, Keenan Wynn, while Hawn downs Valium just to go on a shopping trip with Reynolds' mother and sister. She winds up with an unsightly new hairdo and an unexpected hospital stay.

**Commentary**

In Best Friends, Norman Jewison (director of Diner and The Natural) and writer Valerie Curtin (And Justice for All) wrote a low-key domestic farce about two writers who decide after a period of living together to get married. While Jewison and Curtin failed to create a coherent plot, their characters provided entertaining vehicles for the performers. Jessica Tandy and Barnard Hughes, as Goldie Hawn's parents, are splendid cameo roles as well as Audra Lindley and Keenan Wynn as Reynolds' parents, and Ron Silver as a Hollywood producer who is a compulsive liar.

**Reviews**

New York Times (12-17-82)--The Times found Reynolds and Hawn a "surprisingly appealing" comic team in this low-key farce in which they play with less broad humor and madcap joking than usual. The film freed the two stars from their familiar images and broad performances. The reviewer faulted the film's inconclusive ending with a shot of "two lovers walking into an artificial sunset."

Variety (12-15-82)--The trade paper found Best Friends an "engaging film." It praised the intelligent screenplay about issues faced by newlyweds dealing with themselves, their families and society. Jessica Tandy and Barnard Hughes were praised as the bride's parents with "Tandy wonderfully entertaining as she proceeds in her own little world." The reviewer was taken with the seriousness of the story that followed the progress, decline and eventual revitalization of the Reynolds-Hawn relationship.

*****

**F18 THE WORLD ACCORDING TO GARP**
(Warner Brothers; 1982; 136 minutes; Video: Warner)

**Credits**

Based on the novel by John Irving

| | |
|---|---|
| Director | George Roy Hill |
| Producers | George Roy Hill, Robert L. Crawford |
| Executive Producer | Patrick Kelley |
| Screenplay | Steve Tesich |
| Camera (Technicolor) | Miroslav Ondricek |
| Editor | Stephen A. Rotter |
| Musical Score | David Shire |
| Production Design | Henry Bumstead |
| Art Direction | Woods Mackintosh |
| Set Decoration | Robert Drumheller, Justin Scoppa, Jr. |
| Costume Design | Ann Roth |
| Sound | Chris Newman |
| Animation | John Canemaker |
| Assistant Director | Alan Hopkins |

**Cast**

| | |
|---|---|
| T. S. Garp | Robin Williams |
| Helen Holm | Mary Beth Hurt |
| Jenny Fields | Glenn Glose |
| Roberta Muldoon | John Lithgow |
| Mr. Fields | Hume Cronyn |
| Mrs. Fields | Jessica Tandy |
| Hooker | Swoosie Kurtz |
| Young Garp | James McCall |
| John Wolfe | Peter Michael Goetz |
| Dean Bodger | George Ede |
| Michael Milton | Mark Soper |
| Duncan | Nathan Babcock |
| Walt | Ian MacGregor |
| Stew Percy | Warren Berlinger |
| Midge Percy | Susan Browning |
| Ernie Holm | Brandon Maggart |
| Cushie | Jenny Wright |
| Pooh | Brenda Currin |
| Young Cushie | Jullian Ross |
| Young Pooh | Laurie Robyn |
| Ellen James | Amanda Plummer |
| Stephen | Ron Frazier |
| Rachel | Katherine Borowitz |
| Randy | Harris Laskaway |
| Laurel | Lori Shelle |
| Alice | Kath Reiter |
| Referee | John Irving |

Also: Victor Magnotta, Dominic A. Cerere, Dan Goldman, Christopher Farr, Brett Littman, Brendon Roth, Steven Krey, Al Cerullo, Jr., Matthew C. Materago, Deborah Watkins, Mark Sulton, Bette Henritze, Jeanne DeBaer, Don Frazier, Isabell Mark, Edgard L. Mourino, John S. Corcoran, Tim Gallin, Kate McGregor-Stewart, Sabrina Lee Moore, James Appleby, Matthew Cowles, Eve Gordon, David Fields, Ryan David, Kaiulani Lee, Thomas Peter Daikos, Laura Kaye.

**Synopsis**

A bittersweet tale, adapted from John Irving's novel, portrays a man's growth from childhood to adulthood. Robin Williams as T. S. Garp is almost the solo creation of his mother. In 1944, Glenn Close wants a child but not a husband. While a soldier lay dying of head injuries in a hospital where Close is a nurse, she has sex with him as his last act on earth and becomes pregnant. Her pregnancy shocks her conservative parents, Jessica Tandy and Hume Cronyn. Tandy faints under the stress of Close's disclosure.

Close and her young son move into a boys' preparatory boarding school where she is the school nurse and her son grows up wanting to be a flyer like his father. There are many childhood adventures with dogs, climbing, sports, and pre-pubescent girls. James McCall as the young Garp gives way to Robin Williams who, even as an adolescent, wants to be a writer and an amateur wrestler. Eager to gain experiences that he can write about, Williams meets Mary Beth Hurt, the daughter of his wrestling coach. He tries to impress her with his writing but she ignores him. He turns to another for sex and Hurt learns about the affair and then ignores Williams when he publishes his first short story. Just as he is ready to enter college, his mother finishes her autobiography, "A Sexual Suspect," and finds a publisher.

Time lapses and Williams returns from college as an author who is about to publish his first novel. He is engaged to Hurt. Nevertheless, Close becomes the literary celebrity; her first book is a success and the feminist movement embraces her. Though envious of his mother's success, Williams continues to write and to raise two sons all the while attempting to avoid the "undertoad," the unseen, pervasive threat which lurks everywhere and strikes without warning.

Close's book fosters a movement called the "Ellen Jamesians" that is inspired by the rape and tongue removal of a young woman named Ellen James. Close makes her home a haven for the "Ellen Jamesians" and Williams and family are surrounded by a horde of mute and militant women some of whom have had their tongues removed. John Lithgow, a former football player who is a transsexual, becomes part of the group inhabiting Close's house.

Williams lives nearby with his wife and two sons, Babcock and MacGregor. He tries to teach his sons about life but is limited by his own inability to fathom mortality. Hurt has begun a career as a teacher while Williams continues to write and publish but their relationship rapidly fills with ennui. He has a fling with the eighteen year-old baby sitter and Hurt takes one of her students as a lover. Williams finds out about his wife's affair and is devastated. In breaking off the affair, Hurt agrees to meet Mark Soper, her lover, a final time. Seated in a large Buick in Williams' driveway, Soper pleads with Hurt to have sex with him. She is performing oral sex when Williams arrives with the children in the old Volvo. They are playing a game whereby Williams cuts off the car's headlights and drives in the darkness into their driveway. Not expecting another car, he smashes into the Buick. Hurt bites off Soper's penis, MacGregor is killed, Babcock loses an eye, and both Williams and Hurt are seriously injured.

They convalesce at Close's home where Williams and Lithgow become friends. Close speaks at a political rally on behalf of a feminist candidate and is assassinated. Williams then meets the real "Ellen James," Amanda Plummer, who thanks him for writing a book about her. Williams appears to be happy now and returns to his old school to become the wrestling coach. Brenda Currin, the mature version of the woman who has been his nemesis from the time the young Garp trifled with her sister, walks into the wrestling room and shoots Williams. He survives and flies away with Hurt in a helicopter from the scene of so much pain and injury.

**Commentary**

Despite the excellence of the film and its cast, it was not a huge success. Close was breathtaking as the fanatical mother and the child actors were wonderful. In its multitude of short scenes and close editing, the film bore a closer resemblance to Slaughterhouse Five than to any of George Roy Hill's other movies.

**Reviews**

New York Times (7-23-82)--The Times called the film "gentle, intelligent, and interesting." Concerned about adapting Irving's convoluted novel for film, the reviewer, nevertheless, praised Steve Tesich's screenplay and George Roy Hill's direction as economical and adroit. Robin Williams' performance was described as engaging but erratic.

Variety (7-7-82)--The trade paper also questioned the effort to translate Irving's novel into a satisfying film. Nevertheless, the reviewer praised Glenn Close as a "perfect choice as Jenny Fields," Mary Beth Hurt as Garp's wife, and John Lithgow as the transsexual who created a "moving portrait of a social and sexual misfit."

*****

**F19 THE BOSTONIANS**
(Almi Pictures, Inc.; 1984; 120 minutes; Video: Vestron)

**Credits**

| | |
|---|---|
| Based on the novel by Henry James | |
| Director | James Ivory |
| Producer | Ismail Merchant |
| Assistant Director | David Appleton |
| Screenplay | Ruth Prawer Jhabvala |
| Camera (Color) | Walter Lassally |
| Editors | Katherine Wenning, Mark Potter |
| Musical Score | Richard Robbins |
| Production Design | Leo Austin |
| Art Direction | Tom Walden, Don Carpentier |
| Set Decoration | Richard Elton |
| Costume Design | Jenny Beavan, John Bright |
| Sound | Ray Beckett |
| Assistant Director | David Appleton |

**Cast**

| | |
|---|---|
| Basil Ransome | Christopher Reeves |
| Olive Chancellor | Vanessa Redgrave |
| Verena Tarrant | Madeleine Potter |
| Miss Birdseye | Jessica Tandy |
| Mrs. Burrage | Nancy Marchand |
| Dr. Tarrant | Wesley Addy |
| Mrs. Tarrant | Barbara Bryne |
| Dr. Prance | Linda Hunt |
| Adeline Luna | Nancy New |
| Mr. Pardon | Wallace Shawn |
| Henry Burrage | John Van Ness Philip |
| Henrietta Stackpole | Maura Moynihan |
| Mrs. Farrinder | Martha Farrar |

**Synopsis**

The story revolves around the rivalry between prim, severe idealist Olive Chancellor, Vanessa Redgrave, an intense nineteenth-century feminist and her charmingly cynical Southern cousin Basil Ransome, Christopher Reeves, when they find themselves in competition for the same young woman. The moral ambiguity of Henry James's novel is captured in the struggle between Redgrave and Reeves to possess Madeleine Potter, an innocent young woman whose naive talent for public speaking has drawn her an ardent following. The film ends with Reeves leading the questionably liberated Potter away in marriage from a distraught Redgrave.

**Commentary**

Reviewers said that Vanessa Redgrave was "born to play Olive Chancellor," James's heroine with eyes of "green ice." The entire cast, especially the supporting roles, were praised. Jessica Tandy played the drily sardonic elderly Emersonian Miss Birdseye; Linda Hunt, the new-age "woman" doctor; Nancy Marchand, the pragmatic matron who wants to be Potter's mother-in-law; and Wesley Addy, Potter's faith-healing quack of a father. The extraordinary adaptation was written by Ruth Jahbvala (Shakespeare Wallah, Roseland, Heat and Dust).

**Reviews**

New York Times (8/2/84; 8/8/84)--The Times gave an enthusiastic review to the film, its script and performances. Vanessa Redgrave was called "astonishing" as James's heroine and Jessica Tandy "radiant" as Miss Birdseye, the ancient abolitionist who had been a member of almost every radical cause of her time.

Variety (5-23-84)--The trade paper reprinted a May 14th British review which found the film's distaste for the feminist movement a guarantee to alienate present-day feminists. The reviewer thought Vanessa Redgrave's "traumatized intensity" unpleasant but Madeleine Potter's performance ultimately convincing. Praised for their cameo performances were Jessica Tandy as Miss Birdseye, the elderly believer in "progress"; Linda Hunt as Dr. Prance, the humanistic medic; and Nancy New as Mrs. Luna who pursues Reeves with traditional feminine guile.

*****

**F20** **COCOON**
(20th Century Fox; 1985; 117 minutes; Video: CBS/Fox)

**Credits**

From an unpublished novel by David Saperstein

| | |
|---|---|
| Director | Ron Howard |
| Producers | Richard D. Zanuck, David Brown, Lili Fini Zanuck |
| Associate Producer | Robert Doudel |
| Assistant Director | Jan R. Lloyd |
| Screenplay | Tom Benedek |
| Camera (DeLuxe Color) | Don Peterman |
| Editors | Daniel Hanley, Michael J. Hill |
| Musical Score | James Horner |
| Sound | Richard Church |
| Production Design | Jack T. Collis |
| Costume Design | Aggie Guerard Rodgers |
| Special Visual Effects | Industrial Light & Magic |
| Visual Effects Supervisor | Ken Ralston for ILM |
| Special Creature Effects | Greg Cannom, Robert Short Prods., Rick Baker |

| | |
|---|---|
| Stunt Coordinator | Ted Grossman |
| Special Music and Dance Coordinator | Gwen Verdon |

**Cast**

| | |
|---|---|
| Art Selwyn | Don Ameche |
| Ben Luckett | Wilford Brimley |
| Joe Finley | Hume Cronyn |
| Walter | Brian Dennehy |
| Bernie Lefkowitz | Jack Gilford |
| Jack Bonner | Steve Guttenberg |
| Mary Luckett | Maureen Stapleton |
| Alma Finley | Jessica Tandy |
| Bess McCarthy | Gwen Verdon |
| Rose Lefkowitz | Herta Ware |
| Kitty | Tahnee Welch |
| David | Barret Oliver |
| Susan | Linda Harrison |
| Pillsbury | Tyrone Power, Jr. |
| John Dexter | Clint Howard |
| Pops | Charles Lampkin |
| Doc | Mike Nomad |
| Dectective | Rance Howard |
| Lou Pine | Jorge Gil |
| DMV Clerk | Jim Ritz |
| Smiley | Charles Rainsbury |

**Synopsis**

Cocoon is the story of a miracle by which a group of Florida retirees escape their mortality. Extraterrestial aliens come to Earth in the form of neatly dressed tourists and accidentally restore the elderly people to youthful health and energies.

The film is a fairy tale in which an elderly group is rejuvenated so that they romp about like young adults. Don Ameche, Hume Cronyn, and Wilford Brimley form a trio of swimming buddies who one day discover an unusual change in their favorite pool. An abandoned estate with an indoor pool has been rented by Brian Dennehy who has also charted a boat for himself and his young friends to scuba dive for what appear to be gigantic oyster shells. Soon they bring the large pods back and submerge them in the pool. The three elderly heroes, determined not to let these strange pods spoil their swimming (they sneak away daily from the retirement home and swim in the unattended pool), dive into the pool. They return from their outing sexually rejuvenated, thus delighting their loved ones--Jessica Tandy, Maureen Stapleton, and Gwen Verdon.

The effects of rejuvenation on the three retired couples, the inevitable mania when the whole retirement home wants to go swimming, and the effect on the plans of the space visitors to rescue their own buried in the cocoons propel the film towards a suspenseful, ironic conclusion. Unable to rescue their own, the space visitors rescue the retirement dwellers from the inevitable morbidity of old age.

**Commentary**

Cocoon proved a summer bonanza in 1985, for it tapped a wellspring of universal desires for health and youth. With similarities to Steven Spielberg's E.T. and Close Encounters of The Third Kind, Cocoon is a gentle fantasy tale dealing with the brightening of the lives of elderly people in a final awesome exploration of living.

Jessica Tandy and Hume Cronyn romp through another retirement-home movie as husband and wife. Tandy is cast once again in a minor wifely role that asks little of her talent.

**Reviews**

The New York Times (6-21-85)--The Times reviewer found the cast of veteran stars the film's finest asset. "Given the caliber of the cast," he wrote, "Cocoon can't help being the senior actors' show."

Variety (6-19-85)--The industry's trade paper called the film a "mesmerizing tale" and a "gentle picture that packs a punch." The script (based on the unpublished novel by David Saperstein) and the acting were termed "perfectly focused." Herta Ware's death scene when husband Jack Gilford takes her to the miracle pool in a futile effort to save her life is cited as one of the film's finest moments.

*****

**F21 BATTERIES NOT INCLUDED**
(Universal; 1987; 105 minutes; Video: Vestron)

**Credits**

From a story by Mick Garris

| | |
|---|---|
| Director | Matthew Robbins |
| Producer | Ronald I. Schwary |
| Executive Producers | Steven Spielberg, Kathleen Kennedy, Frank Marshall |
| Screenplay | Brad Bird, Matthew Robbins, Brent Maddock, S. S. Wilson |
| Camera | John McPherson |
| Editor | Cynthia Scheider |
| Musical Score | James Horner |
| Production Design | Ted Haworth |
| Sound | Gene Cantamessa, Shawn Graham |
| Art Direction | Angelo Graham |
| Set Decoration | George R. Nelson |
| Costumes | Aggie Guerard Rodgers |
| Special Effects | Ken Pepiot |

| | |
|---|---|
| Visual Effects | Bruce Nicholson |
| Makeup | Rick Sharp |
| Stunt Coordinator | Thomas Rosales |

**Cast**

| | |
|---|---|
| Frank | Hume Cronyn |
| Faye | Jessica Tandy |
| Harry | Frank McRae |
| Marisa | Elizabeth Pena |
| Carlos | Michael Carmine |
| Mason | Dennis Boutsikaris |
| Sid | Tom Aldredge |
| Muriel | Jane Hoffman |
| Gus | John DiSanti |
| Kovacs | John Pankow |
| DeWitt | MacIntrye Dixon |
| Lacey | Michael Greene |
| Mrs. Thompson | Doris Belack |
| Pamela | Wendy Schaal |

Also: Jose Santana, James Le Gross, Ronald Schwary, Susan Shoffner, Shelly Kurtz, Joseph Hamer, H. Clay Dear, Howard Renensland, Judy Grafe, Alice Beardsley, Dick Martinsen, Charles Raymond, Riki Colon, Jon Imparato, David Vasquez, John Arceri.

Synopsis

A sci-fi film in which flying saucers arrive in a soon-to-be-demolished East Village tenement in Manhattan. The various residents that provide the film's interest are types: the starving artist, the hoodlum with a heart of gold, the unwed pregnant woman, the kindly superintendent, and a beleagured restaurant owner and his dotty wife played by Hume Cronyn and Jessica Tandy. The tenement building, slated to be demolished by a ruthless builder who wants the property for his skyscraper complex, stands alone amid a city block of bulldozed rubble. Cronyn and his friends resist eviction but they are brutalized by a gang of neighborhood thugs who are paid to smash their resistance. At the end of a day that has seen Cronyn's restaurant destroyed, he sits down at his kitchen table and says to himself, "Please somebody help us." And, a pair of flying saucers, no bigger than a Frisbee, arrives. These "little guys" with tiny headlights and mechanical limbs eat metal, reproduce and recharge themselves by plugging into a household electrical outlet. In an instant, they magically repair all the damage done by the thugs. The speculator attempts to blow-up the building. Tandy narrowly escapes as the building collapses and a disconsolate Cronyn surveys the ruins surrounded by a massed force of saucers. The next day, the building has miraculously been restored, the speculator gives up, and everyday life is resumed.

**Commentary**

This Hollywood fantasy is rooted in the harsh reality of those surviving in abandoned buildings used as havens for drug dealers. Though many of our urban structures have been rehabilitated as condos, the question remains what happens to the previous inhabitants--the elderly, the poor, and Latino?

Batteries Not Included takes after Cocoon by making its protagonists elderly rather than young and permits then to triump over the corrupting forces of progress with the help of extraterrestrials.

**Reviews**

New York Times (12-18-87)--The Times reviewer found the humans far more interesting than the mechanical creatures with the wistful eyes in this fantasy. Of Jessica Tandy who "acts with a sense of fun," the reviewer said that she was a charmingly dotty woman "whose senility seems to have left her in a state of grace."

New York Post (12-18-87)--The reviewer credited Tandy and Cronyn with rescuing this film from appearing to be a retread of E. T., Cocoon, and Short Circuit with its playful aliens, extraterrestrial forces that make life joyful for old people, and machines that take on human personalities.

*****

**F22 THE HOUSE ON CARROLL STREET**
(Orion; 1988; 101 minutes; Video: HBO)

**Credits**

| | |
|---|---|
| Producer/Director | Peter Yates |
| Screenplay | Walter Bernstein |
| Co-Producer | Robert F. Colesberry |
| Executive Producers | Arlene Donovan, Robert Benton |
| Music | Georges Delerue |
| Editor | Ray Lovejoy |
| Photography | Michael Ballhaus |
| Production Design | Stuart Wurtzel |
| Costume Design | Rita Ryack |
| Art Direction | W. Steven Graham |
| Set Decoration | George DeTitta, Jr. |
| Sound | Tod Maitland |
| Associate Producer | Nellie Nugiel |
| Production Manager | Thomas A. Razzano |
| Assistant Director | Joseph Reidy |

**Cast**

| | |
|---|---|
| Emily Crane | Kelly McGillis |
| Cochran | Jeff Daniels |
| Ray Salwen | Mandy Patinkin |
| Miss Venable | Jessica Tandy |
| Alan | Jonathan Hogan |
| Senator Byington | Remak Ramsay |
| Hackett | Ken Welsh |
| Stefan | Christopher Rhode |
| Salwen Aides | Charles McCaughan, Randle Mell |
| Senator | Michael Flanagan |
| Randolph Slote | Paul Sparer |
| Warren | Brian Davies |
| Maid | Mary Diveny |
| Teperson | Bill Moor |
| Woman in the house | Patricia Falkenhain |
| FBI Director | Frederick Rolf |
| Funeral Woman | Anna Berger |
| McKay | Cliff Cudney |
| Sackadorf | Alexis Yulin |
| Lieutenant Sloan | Trey Wilson |
| FBI Librarian | William Duff-Griffin |
| Conductor | George Ede |
| Gateman | John Carpenter |
| Porter | Jamey Sheridan |
| Barber | P. J. Barry |
| Hurwitz | Boris Leskin |
| Bistrong | Marat Yusim |
| The Official | James Rebhorn |
| Boria | Howard Sherman |
| Agent Simpson | John Randolph Jones |
| Stage Manager | David Hart |
| Mrs. Byington | Maeve McGuire |
| Senator Byington's Daughter | Suzanne Slade |
| Senator Byington's Son | Todd DeFreitas |

Also: Charles McCaughan, Randle Mell, Patricia Falkenhain, Anna Berger, John Carpenter, Jamey Sheridan, P. J. Barry, Gregory Jbara, Polly O'Malley, Maureen Moore, Alice Drummond, Daniel Mills, Jim Babchak

**Synopsis**

The House on Carroll Street is set in a romantic urban landscape where New York City is beautiful and clean and the subways are safe. The peaceful setting is at odds with the sinister political climate of 1951 in which McCarthyism is at work. The opening scene shows a young Life magazine photo editor Emily Crane (Kelly McGillis) being interrogated by a Senate committee whose chief counsel is a vaguely Roy Cohn-ish figure played by Mandy Patinkin. She belongs to a liberal group and Patinkin demands that she name her colleagues and reminds her that the photographs she selects for Life magazine are "information received by millions of unsuspecting Americans." She refuses to cooperate, is charged with contempt of Congress, and the next day loses her job. The film's atmosphere of paranoia and fear is thus established.

To support herself, McGillis answers a newspaper advertisement for an individual to read to an elderly woman with failing eyesight. It just happens that Miss Venable's (Jessica Tandy) house looks out upon a courtyard and the rear of houses on a parallel street--Carroll Street. The first day on the job, McGillis sees a suspicious scene through a rear window involving furtive-looking foreigners and her nemesis from the Senate committee (Mandy Patinkin). In the meantime, two F.B.I. men make life difficult for her by searching her apartment and interviewing her new employer. Tandy, ever the eccentric, dismisses the FBI inquiry and retains her reader for purely selfish reasons.

Not content with observing the suspicious scene, McGillis proceeds to investigate and blunders into life-threatening intrigues from which she is saved again and again by the two F.B.I. agents. She becomes romantically involved with one (Jeff Daniels) after he saves her from a bomb blast. One adventure after another follows until they solve the mystery: Nazi scientists are being infiltrated into the United States by right-wing politicians using immigration permits of dead German Jews. The film's climax is a battle between the forces of good and evil across the upper reaches of Grand Central Terminal. Daniels and McGillis are saved but not for each other. He is transferred to the Northwest and they decide their relationship is a mix of "oil and water" and she stays in New York.

**Commentary**

The House on Carroll Street was filmed in 1986 but not released until 1988. Intended as a romantic thriller, some scenes are reminiscent of Alfred Hitchcock's Rear Window. Kelly McGillis reads stories to a wealthy elderly woman, played by Jessica Tandy, and spies something suspicious in the house across the way involving German-speaking foreigners and the Roy Cohn-like figure who earlier tormented her before a Senate investigating committee. Tandy's performance as Miss Venable, an abrupt, eccentric elderly woman, barely received comment from reviewers.

**Reviews**

New York Times (4-4-88)--Janet Maslin, writing for The Times, called The House on Carroll Street a silly suspense story speeding breathlessly from one wild coincidence to another.

Variety (3-2-88)--The Variety reviewer dismissed the film as a Nancy Drew thriller set in New York City in which the grown-up sleuth trailed improbable characters involved in ridiculous conspiracies.

*****

**F23 COCOON: THE RETURN**
(20th Century Fox; 1988; 116 minutes; Video: Fox)

**Credits**

| | |
|---|---|
| Based on a story by | Stephen McPherson and Elizabeth Bradley |
| Based on characters | created by David Saperstein |
| Director | Daniel Petrie |
| Producer | Richard D. Zanuck, David Brown, Lili Fini Zanuck |
| Screenplay | Stephen McPherson |
| Camera (Deluxe color) | Tak Fujimoto |
| Editor | Mark Roy Warner |
| Music | James Horner |
| Production Design | Lawrence G. Pauli |
| Set Decoration | Frederick C. Weiler, Jim Poynter |
| Costume Design | Jay Hurley |
| Cocoon Designer | Robert Short |
| Visual Effects | Industrial Light & Magic |
| Special Effects | I. B. Jones |
| Sound | Hank Garfield |
| Associate Producer | Gary Daigler |
| Assistant Director | Katterli Frauenfelder |
| Casting | Beverly McDermott |

**Cast**

| | |
|---|---|
| Art Selwyn | Don Ameche |
| Ben Luckett | Wilford Brimley |
| Joe Finley | Hume Cronyn |
| Bernie Lefkowitz | Jack Gilford |
| Jack Bonner | Steve Guttenberg |
| David | Barret Oliver |
| Mary Luckett | Maureen Stapleton |
| Alma Finley | Jessica Tandy |
| Bess McCarthy | Gwen Verdon |
| Ruby | Elaine Stritch |
| Sara | Courteney Cox |

**Synopsis**

The three elderly couples that escaped to Antarea in Cocoon have returned to earth for a four-day visit. They are still enjoying a resurgence of youth. The reason for their return is vague ("unfinished business"). They are reunited with family and friends and each questions his choice for leaving in the first place. The geriatric renegades appear on the doorstep of Bernie Lefkowitz (Jack Gilford), a widower who elected not to go with them to Antarea. He is now learning to hook rugs in an old-age home. The friends decide to help Gilford shake off his gloom. His elderly buddies strike up a volleyball game with young girls at the beach but Gilford mopes about in his streetclothes and takes his friends to the cemetery to visit his wife's grave. Eventually, Gilford is wooed by a brassy motel operator (Elaine Stritch) who does everything she can to banish the blues.

The Lucketts (Wilford Brimley and Maureen Stapleton) become reacquainted with their daughter and grandson; another couple faces a life-threatening illness. The younger characters of Cocoon reappear as the tour boat operator (Steve Guttenberg) and there are scientists, led by Courteney Cox, who study a silent, glowing cocoon that is slowly dying in the hands of experiment-happy scientists.

The characters' dilemma is whether they wish to return to eternal youth on the problem-free planet or linger on Earth with friends, families, and the prospect of mortality.

**Commentary**

Cocoon: The Return falls into the pattern of sequels whose "return" is not as successful as the original. This sequel is blessed with the presence of the original "senior" actors, including Tandy-Cronyn, Ameche-Verdon, Brimley-Stapleton, and Jack Gilford whose cranky, morose character succeeds in developing a new direction (with Elaine Stritch). The other duos are asked to repeat their earlier "youthful" antics.

**Reviews**

New York Times (11-23-88)--Janet Maslin of The Times dismissed the sequel to Cocoon as "so tired it can barely recapitulate the winning formula of the original hit."

Variety (11-23-88)--The Variety reviewer found the sequel less enjoyable than Cocoon and called the film an overdose of bathos resulting in a maudlin rather than magic effort.

*****

**F24 DRIVING MISS DAISY**
(Warner; 1989; 99 minutes; Video: Warner)

**Credits**

Based on the play by Alfred Uhry

| | |
|---|---|
| Director | Bruce Beresford |
| Producers | Richard D. Zanuck, Lili Fini Zanuck |
| Executive Producer | David Brown |
| Screenplay | Alfred Uhry |
| Photography | Peter James |
| Production Design | Bruno Rubeo |
| Art Direction | Victor Kempster |
| Music | Hans Zimmer |

| | |
|---|---|
| Editor | Mark Warner |
| Costumes | Elizabeth McBride |
| Coexecutive Producer | Jake Eberts |
| Associate Producers | Robert Doudell, Alfred Uhry |
| Assistant Director | Katterli Frauenfelder |

**Cast**

| | |
|---|---|
| Hoke Colburn | Morgan Freeman |
| Daisy Werthan | Jessica Tandy |
| Boolie Werthan | Dan Aykroyd |
| Florine Werthan | Patti LuPone |
| Idella | Esther Rolle |
| Miss McClatchey | Joann Havrilla |
| Oscar | William Hall, Jr. |
| Dr. Weil | Alvin M. Sugarman |
| Nonie | Clarice F. Geigerman |
| Miriam | Muriel Moore |
| Beulah | Sylvia Kaler |
| Neighbor Lady | Carolyn Gold |
| Katie Bell | Crystal R. Fox |
| Red Mitchell | Bob Hannah |
| Troopers | Ray McKinnon, Ashley Josey |
| Slick | Jack Rousso |
| Insurance Agent | Fred Faser |
| Soloist | Indra A. Thomas |

**Synopsis**

The film begins with Miss Daisy (Jessica Tandy) inching her black Cadillac out of her Atlanta driveway when suddenly the car zooms backward across the flower beds and retaining wall to dangle exposed over the neighbor's yard. Miss Daisy has put her foot on the gas pedal instead of the brake, though she says, "That car misbehaved." Her son Boolie (Dan Aykroyd) has the good sense not to accuse his seventy-year old mother of the obvious but proceeds to employ a driver for her. Against her furious objection he hires Hoke Colburn (Morgan Freeman), a black man in his sixties. Hoke is a widower who has infinite patience, tact, and vast reserves of subversive wit.

Thus begins the story of a remarkable 25-year friendship between Miss Daisy and her black chauffeur that chronicles the social changes taking place in the South between 1948 and 1973. On one side is Miss Daisy, the rich Jewish widow who hates being called rich and loathes the idea of servants. She tolerates her cook and housekeeper Idelia (Esther Rolle) who, in turn, tolerates her. On the other side is Hoke who knows more of the real world and his "place" in it than Miss Daisy. To Hoke's amusement, Miss Daisy clings to the memories of her humble beginnings on the wrong side of the tracks and to her years as a schoolteacher. The small moments that solidify the relationship begin with Miss Daisy accusing Hoke of stealing a tin of salmon only to have him arrive for work with another tin to put in the place of the one he had eaten; she teaches Hoke how to read and he teaches her about the world he inhabits as a person of color; they drive to Mobile to see Miss Daisy's relatives only to be stopped by state troopers who are suspicious of a black man and a white woman being together; they grieve over the bombing of Atlanta's Jewish temple; and despite her son's distress Miss Daisy attends a speech delivered in Atlanta by Dr. Martin Luther King only to hurt Hoke's feelings by not inviting him to attend.

Miss Daisy's family includes her son and his nouveau riche wife Florine (Patti LuPone) whose idea of heaven, according to Miss Daisy, is "socializing with Episcopalians." As successful members of Atlanta's business community, they are intent upon disguising their uniqueness as a Jewish minority.

The passage of years brings the film to its poignant close. Miss Daisy's world changes: Idelia dies of a stroke while shelling peas in Miss Daisy's kitchen, Hoke becomes too old to drive, Miss Daisy can no longer stay by herself in the large house and is placed in a nursing home. In the final scene, Hoke is taken by his granddaughter to visit Miss Daisy and since she is too frail and distracted to feed herself, he helps her with her food in the dining room of the nursing home.

**Commentary**

Alfred Uhry sold the film rights to his Pulitzer Prize-winning play in 1987. Australian director Bruce Beresford had previously filmed Beth Henley's Crimes of the Heart and Horton Foote's Tender Mercies--two Southern plays. Having secured the rights to Driving Miss Daisy, he hired Uhry to write the filmscript which chronicles the cantankerous yet poignant friendship between Miss Daisy and her chauffeur and filmed it in the Druid Hills section of Atlanta. Morgan Freeman was an easy choice since he originated the role of Hoke on the New York stage. However, Beresford was insistent that Miss Daisy should be played by an actress either "the right age for the role or in easy reach of it" and resisted a number of actresses in their late 40s and early 50s. Just as the film was released, Jessica Tandy, whom Uhry has called "a national treasure," turned eighty years old.

**Reviews**

New York Times (12-13-89)--Vincent Canby, writing for The Times, called the film a "chamber piece from the stage" and praised it as a small, pure and healthily skeptical chronicle of social changes taking play in the South between 1948 and 1973. Canby remarked that in her long career in films Tandy had never had a film role of the richness and humor to match Miss Daisy. "She brings to it her mastery of what might be called selective understatement," he added.

# Television Appearances

## Principal Television Appearances

**T01** Portrait of a Madonna (9-26-48; ABC-TV; 30 minutes)

One of the first "prestige" dramatic showcases on the fledging ABC network and produced live each week by the Actors Studio, Inc., with host Marc Connelly and producer Donald Davis. The one-act play, Portrait of a Madonna, by Tennessee Williams was the first telecast in this series, starring Jessica Tandy.

**T02** Masterpiece Playhouse (7-23-50 to 9-3-50; NBC-TV; 60 minutes)

Live productions of seven great classics, including Ibsen's Hedda Gabler and Shakespeare's Richard III. Appearing in these productions were Jessica Tandy, William Windom, and Boris Karloff.

**T03** Omnibus (10-4-53 to 3-31-57; CBS-TV; 90 minutes)

In the its first season, Omnibus presented dramatic plays based on works by William Inge, James Thurber, Carson McCullers, Ernest Hemingway, and John Steinbeck with such performers as Jessica Tandy, Hume Cronyn, Carol Channing, Walter Slezak, Helen Hayes, Claude Rains, and E. G. Marshall. In addition, Omnibus, one of the longest-running cultural series in the history of commercial network television, presented (without commercials) opera, symphony, ballet, dramatic plays, and true-life adventure films. First produced on CBS and then on ABC.

**T04** The Marriage (7-8-54 to 8-19-54; NBC-TV; 30 minutes)

Jessica Tandy and Hume Cronyn starred in this comedy-drama series set in New York City about life in the close-knit Marriott family, including Ben, an attorney; his wife, Liz; and their children, Emily and Peter. This comedy was the first network series to be regularly telecast in color. Cronyn and Tandy had starred in the NBC radio version of this series which had left the air in the Spring of 1954.

Cast

| | |
|---|---|
| Ben Marriott | Hume Cronyn |
| Liz Marriott | Jessica Tandy |
| Emily Marriott | Susan Strasberg |
| Peter Marriott | Malcolm Brodrick |
| Bobby Logan | William Redfield |

**T05** Christmas 'Til Closing (12-18-55; NBC-TV)

A Philco Playhouse episode.

**T06** The Fourposter (1955; NBC-TV)

Tandy created her role of Agnes in the television adaptation of Jan de Hartog's play with Hume Cronyn.

**T07** The Moon and Sixpence (10-30-59; NCB-TV; 90 minutes)

Tandy as Blanche Stroeve in an adaptation of Somerset Maugham's novel with Laurence Olivier, Judith Anderson, Denholm Elliott, Hume Cronyn, Cyril Cusack, Geraldine Fitzgerald.

**T08** The Fallen Idol-Dupont Show of the Month (10-14-59; NCB-TV)

**T09** Long Distance (3-31-60 to 9-22-60; NBC-TV; 30 minutes)

Jessica Tandy, Isobel Elsom, and Carl Benton Reid star in a television drama titled "Producers' Choice" centered on a wife's discovery minutes before her husband's scheduled execution of a letter that proves his innocence. The story concerns her hysteria as she tries to reach the governor to obtain a reprieve.

**T10** Tennessee Williams' South (12-73; CBC-TV; 80 minutes)

A documentary, produced and directed by Harry Rasky for the Canadian Broadcasting Corporation, about the South of Tennessee Williams plus excerpts from his plays. Jessica Tandy performs one of Blanche DuBois' speeches from A Streetcar Named Desire. Performers include Jessica Tandy, Burl Ives, Colleen Dewhurst, Michael York, John Colicos, Maureen Stapleton, William Hutt, and Tennessee Williams as himself.

**T11** Many Faces of Love (1977; CBS-TV)

Tandy and Cronyn reading a series of scenes from Tennessee Williams' plays.

**T12** The Gin Game (1979; PBS 3-6-84)

Tandy recreated her role of Fonsia Dorsey in the play by D. L. Coburn with Hume Cronyn.

**T13** Foxfire (1987; CBS-TV)

Tandy recreated her role of Annie Nations in the Hallmark Hall of Fame production of the play with Hume Cronyn.

**T14** The Story Lady (1991; NBC-TV)

Tandy appeared in the title role with daughter Tandy Cronyn in a supporting role.

**T15** **Other Appearances**

Icebound--Prudential Family Playhouse (1-30-51; CBS-TV)
Hangman's House--Studio One (3-19-51; CBS-TV)
Glory in the Flower--Omnibus (10-4-53; CBS-TV)
John Quincy Adams--Omnibus (1-23-55; CBS-TV)
The End of Blackbeard the Pirate--TV Reader's Digest (7-25-55; ABC-TV)
The Great Adventure--U. S. Steel Hour (1-18-56; CBS-TV)
The School Mistress--Star Stage (2-17-56; NBC-TV)
The Better Half--Omnibus (3-11-56; CBS-TV)
The Confidence Man--Alcoa Hour (5-27-56; NBC-TV)
Toby--Alfred Hitchcock Presents (11-4-56; CBS-TV)
A Murder Is Announced--Goodyear Playhouse (12-30-56; CBS-TV)
The Five Dollar Bill--Studio One (1-21-57; CBS-TV)
Clothes Make the Man--Schlitz Playhouse of Stars (4-5-57; CBS-TV)
Little Miss Bedford--Studio 57 (6-9-57; NN-TV)
The Glass Eye--Alfred Hitchcock Presents (10-6-57; CBS-TV)
Murder Me Gently--Suspicion (10-7-57; NBC-TV)

War Against War--Telephone Time (3-4-58; ABC-TV)
The Canary Sedan--Alfred Hitchcock Presents (6-15-58; CBS-TV)
Glass Flowers Never Drop Petals--Breaking Point (3-23-64; ABC-TV)
Punishments, Cruel and Unusual--Judd for the Defense (12-6-68; ABC-TV)
U. S. Treasury--O'Hara (2-4-72; CBS-TV)
The Set-Up--FBI (2-13-72; ABC-TV)
Onstage: 25 Years at the Guthrie (1988; syndicated)

# Discography

The following is an alphabetical list of the albums recorded by Jessica Tandy. For indexing purposes, the Discography entry number (i.e., **D01**) is listed on the far left side of each entry. It is followed by the name of the recording, then the releasing company and the year of release in parentheses, and finally the manufacturer order number

**D01** Butley (Caedmon Records) TRS 362, CDL5 362, LC 73-751013

A soundtrack recording of the play by British playwright, Simon Gray, featuring Alan Bates and Jessica Tandy. Also in the cast are: Richard O'Callaghan, Susan Engel, Michael Byrne, Georgina Hale, Simon Rouse, John Savident, Oliver Maguire, Colin Haigh, Darien Angadi, Susan Woodridge, Lindsay Ingram, Patti Love, and Belinda Low. Directed by Harold Pinter.

**D02** The Cherry Orchard (Theatre Recording Society; 1966) TRS 314-S

A recording of a play by Anton Chekhov in English translation by Tyrone Guthrie and Leonid Kipnis. A Tyrone Guthrie Production stars Jessica Tandy as Lyobov Ranevskaya, Hume Cronyn as Yepihodov, Lee Richardson as Lopahin, Ruth Nelson as Charlotta, Nancy Wickwire as Varya, and the Minnesota Theatre Company, including Robert Pastene, Kristina Callahan, Ken Ruta, Paul Ballantyne, Ed Flanders, Sandy McCallum and Ellen Geer. Directed by Tyrone Guthrie.

**D03** Coriolanus (Shakespeare Recording Society; 1962) SRS-M 226

This recording of Shakespeare's tragedy stars Richard Burton in the title role and Jessica Tandy as Volumnia. Also in the cast are Michael Hordern as Agrippa, Kenneth Haigh as Aufidicus, Robert Stephens as Brutus with Martin Benson, Douglas Wilmer, Michael Gwynn, Llewellyn Rees, John Gayford, Neil Robinson, Eric Corrie, John Magnus, Robert Seagrave, Alan Browning, Colin Watson, Tarn Bassett, Audrey Fairfax, Lynn Gordon, and others.

**D04** The Glass Menagerie (Caedmon Records; 1964) TRS-M 301

A recording of Tennessee Williams' play with Jessica Tandy as Amanda Wingfield, Montgomery Cliff as Tom, Julie Harris as Laura, and David Wayne as the Gentleman Caller. Directed by Howard Sackler.

**D05** Heartbreak House (Caedmon Records; 1968) TRS-335

The Shaw Festival, Niagara-on-the-Lake, Canada, 1968 production starring Jessica Tandy as Hesione Hushabye, Tony Van Bridge as Captain Shotover, and Paton Whitehead as Hector Hushabye. Others in the cast are: Frances Hyland, Bill Fraser, Eleanor Beecroft, Diana LeBlanc, Patrick Boxill, James Valentine, and Kenneth Wickes. Directed by Val Gielgud.

**D06** Stars Over Broadway (Star-Tone; 1947) ST-214

A compilation LP made from a 1947 radio recording with Jessica Tandy reading a four-minute scene from A Streetcar Named Desire.

**D07** Theatre Guild on the Air (CBS; 1943)

From a radio anthology program also called The U. S. Steel Hour. Jessica Tandy and Charles Laughton read "Payment Deferred."

**D08** The Wind in the Willows. Vol. 2 (Pathways of Sound) No. 1026

"The Open Road" and "Mr. Toad" read by Jessica Tandy and Hume Cronyn from the story by Kenneth Grahame.

**D09** The Wind in the Willows. Vol. 4 (Pathways of Sound) No. 1030

"Toad's Adventures and Further Adventures" read by Jessica Tandy and Hume Cronyn from the story by Kenneth Grahame.

# Awards and Nominations

## Antoinette Perry "Tony" Awards

**A01** A Streetcar Named Desire (1948)

Jessica Tandy wins:
Best Actress in a Play

Other Wins for the Play:
Pulitzer Prize

Other Awards for Tandy:
Drama League Award of New York
Twelfth Night Club Award
Delia Austria Medal

**A02** The Gin Game (1978)

Jessica Tandy wins:
Best Actress in a Play

Other Wins for the Play:
Pulitzer Prize

Other Awards for Tandy (1979):
Drama Desk Award
Chicago's Sarah Siddons Award
Los Angeles Drama Critics Circle Award
National Press Club Award

**A03** Rose (1981)

Nomination for Tandy:
Best Actress in a Supporting Role

**A04** Foxfire (1983)

Jessica Tandy wins:
Best Actress in a Play

Other Awards for Tandy:
Drama Desk Award
Outer Circle Critics Award

**A05** The Petition (1986)

Nomination for Tandy:
Best Actress in a Play

**Oscar**
**(Academy of Motion Pictures and Sciences Award)**

**A06** Driving Miss Daisy (1989)

Jessica Tandy wins:
Best Actress

Other Wins for the film:
Best Picture
Screen Adaptation
Makeup

**Obie**
**(The Village Voice Off-Broadway Award)**

**A07** Not I and Happy Days (1973)

Jessica Tandy wins:
Outstanding Achievement in the Off-Broadway Theatre for Not I (1973)
Distinguished Performance for Not I (1973)

Other Wins for Tandy:
Drama Desk Award for Happy Days and Not I (1973)

**Emmy**
**(Television)**

**A08** Foxfire--Hallmark Hall of Fame (CBS; 1988)

Jessica Tandy Wins:
Best Dramatic Actress in a Television Special

**A09** **Other Awards for Jessica Tandy**

Commoedia Matinee Club Bronze Medallion Award (with Hume Cronyn) for The Fourposter (1952)

Delia Austrian Award from the New York Drama League for Five Finger Exercise (1960)
Leland Powers Honorary Award for A Delicate Balance (1966)
Creative Arts Award from Brandeis University for a Lifetime of Distinguished Achievement (1978)
Inducted into the Theatre Hall of Fame in recognition of outstanding contributions to the American Theatre (1979)
The Common Wealth Award for Distinguished Service in Dramatic Arts (1983)
The John F. Kennedy Center Honors (1986)
Alley Theatre Award for Significant Contributions to the Theatre Arts (1987)
Academy of Science Fiction, Fantasy and Horror Films Award for Best Actress in Batteries not Included (1987)
Franklin Haven Sargent Award (with Hume Cronyn) from the American Academy of Dramatic Arts for Outstanding Quality of Acting (1988)
National Medal of Arts Award (1990)
Theatre LA Annual Ovation Award for Artists Demonstrating a Long-Term Commitment to Los Angeles (1991)

## A10 Honorary Degrees

LL.D., University of Western Ontario, Canada (1974)
L.H.D., Fordham University, New York (1985)

# Bibliography

**BOOKS**

**B01** Atkinson, Brooks. Broadway. Revised Edition. New York: Macmillan, 1974.
Brief summary of the Cronyns' careers as a theatrical team.

**B02** Atkinson, Brooks and Albert Hirschfeld. The Lively Years 1920-1973. New York: Association Press, 1973.
Commentary on A Streetcar Named Desire with Hirschfeld drawing of Tandy and Brando.

**B03** Benson, Eugene and L. W. Conolly. English-Canadian Theatre. Toronto: Oxford University Press, 1987.
Brief mention of Larry Fineberg's Eve with Tandy at the Stratford Festival Theatre in the 1976 season.

**B04** The Biographical Encyclopaedia and Who's Who of the American Theatre. New York: James H. Heineman, 1966.
Includes biographical entry on Tandy.

**B05** Blum, Daniel. A Pictorial History of the American Theatre: 1860-1985. 6th Edition. New York: Crown Publishers, 1986.
Contains 16 production photos of Tandy in plays from Time and the Conways to The Glass Menagerie.

**B06** Blum, Daniel. Theatre World 1947-1948. Vol. 4. New York: D. C. Blum, 1948.
Includes cast and crew data on A Streetcar Named Desire.

B07 Bordman, Gerald. The Oxford Companion to American Theatre. New York: Oxford University Press, 1984.
Includes short biographical sketch on Tandy.

B08 Bronner, Edwin, J. The Encyclopedia of the American Theatre. San Diego, CA: A. S. Barnes, 1980.
Includes short biographical sketch on Tandy.

B09 Brooks, Tim and Earle Marsh. The Complete Directory to Prime Time Network TV Shows, 1946-Present. 4th Edition. New York: Ballantine Books, 1988.
Contains entries on Tandy's television work between 1948 and 1954.

B10 Brustein, Robert. Seasons of Discontent: Dramatic Opinions 1959-1965. New York: Simon and Schuster, 1965.
Includes a discussion of the first season of the Tyrone Guthrie Theater, Minneapolis, with Jessica Tandy and Hume Cronyn in the company.

B11 The Cambridge Guide to World Theatre. Ed. Martin Banham. New York: Cambridge University Press, 1988.
Includes short biographical entry on Tandy.

B12 Celebrity Register 1973. New York: Harper & Row, 1973.
Entries on Tandy are found in the 1959, 1963, and 1973 editions.

B13 A Concise Encyclopedia of the Theatre. 1974.
Includes brief biographical entry on Tandy.

B14 Contemporary Theatre, Film, and Television: A Biographical Guide. Edited by Linda S. Hubbard and Owen O'Donnell. Vol. 7. Detroit, MI: Gale Research Inc., 1989.
Contains lengthy biographical entry on Tandy.

B15 Cottrell, John. Laurence Olivier. Englewood Cliffs, NJ: Prentice-Hall, 1975.
Contains quotes from Tandy on Laurence Olivier's performance as Malcolm in Macbeth with England's Birmingham Repertory Theatre and as Sir Toby Belch in the Old Vic production of Twelfth Night.

B16 Current Biography Yearbook, 1956. Ed. Marjorie Dent Candee. New York: H. W. Wilson, 1956.
Includes biographical entry on Tandy.

**B17** Current Biography Yearbook 1984. Ed. Charles Moritz. New York: H. W. Wilson Company, 1984.
Includes lengthy biographical entry on Tandy.

**B18** Devlin, Albert J., ed. Conversations with Tennessee Williams. Jackson: University Press of Mississippi, 1986.
Tennessee Williams is quoted as saying Tandy was one of his "favorite" actresses.

**B19** Duncan, Barry. The St. James's Theatre: Its Strange & Complete History 1935-1957.
Includes entry on Yes, My Darling Daughter with Tandy as "delightful as the charming blue-stocking Ellen."

**B20** Eames, John Douglas. The MGM Story: The Complete History of Fifty-Seven Roaring Years. Second revised edition. New York: Sundial Publications Ltd., 1986.
Panoramic history of MGM films includes listings of Tandy's MGM films The Seventh Cross, The Valley of Decision, The Green Years.

**B21** Edwards, Anne. Vivien Leigh. New York: Simon & Schuster, 1977.
Brief discussion of the difference between the costumes worn by Tandy in the New York production of A Streetcar Named Desire and those designed for Vivien Leigh for the London production directed by Laurence Olivier.

**B22** Enciclopedia dello spettacolo. Volume 9. Rome: Casa Editrice le Maschere, 1962.
Includes biographical entry on Tandy.

**B23** Forsyth, James. Tyrone Guthrie: A Biography. London: Hamish Hamilton, 1976.
Description of Guthrie's efforts to found a new theatre for repertory in the United States. The theatre was founded in Minneapolis in 1963 and at the heart of that first company were actors of "strength, experience, intelligence and female beauty"--Hume Cronyn, Jessica Tandy, and Zoe Caldwell. Tandy played Gertrude to George Grizzard's Hamlet in the theatre's opening production.

**B24** Forty Years of Screen Credits 1929-1969. Ed. John T. Weaver. Vol. 2. Metuchen, NJ: The Scarecrow Press, 1970.
The entry on Tandy lists 13 film credits.

**B25** Franks, Don. Tony, Grammy, Emmy, Country: A Broadway, Television, and Records Awards

Reference. Jefferson, NC: McFarland and Co., 1986.
Contains entries on Tandy's "Tony" awards from 1948 to 1983.

**B26** A George Jean Nathan Reader. Edited by A. L. Lazarus. Toronto: Associated University Presses, 1990.
Contains a brief biographical note on Tandy.

**B27** Gielgud, John. Early Stages. Revised Edition. London: Hodder & Stoughton, 1987.
Gielgud writes of his 1934 production of Hamlet and comments that "Jessica Tandy's Ophelia was dismissed as a complete failure by certain critics and highly praised by others."

**B28** Gielgud, John with John Miller and John Pavell. Gielgud: An Actor and His Time. A Memoir. New York: Clarkson N. Potter, Inc., 1979.
Gielgud's writings on his career include mention of his work with Jessica Tandy on London's West End and at the Old Vic during the 1930s and 1940s.

**B29** Guernsey, Otis L., Jr. Curtain Times: The New York Theatre: 1965-1987. New York: Applause Theatre Books, 1987.
Comprehensive listing of New York theatre seasons from 1964-65 to 1987. Tandy's Broadway performances are included.

**B30** Guinness, Alec. Blessings in Disguise. New York: Alfred A. Knopf, 1986.
Discussion of John Gielgud directing the cast of Hamlet for the West End in 1934 with Tandy as Ophelia and of Twelfth Night at the Old Vic with Laurence Olivier and Tandy directed by Tyrone Guthrie.

**B31** Guthrie, Tyrone. Minneapolis Rehearsals: Tyrone Guthrie Directs Hamlet. Berkeley: University of California Press, 1970.
See **B64** for description.

**B32** Halliwell, Leslie. The Filmgoer's Companion. 8th Edition. New York: Charles Scribner's, 1984.
Contains entry on Tandy.

**B33** Hammond, David. "Jessica Tandy." Notable Women in the American Theatre. Edited by Alice Robinson, Vera M. Roberts, and Milly S. Barranger. Westport, CT: Greenwood Press, 1989.
Includes a lengthy biographical entry on Tandy.

B34 Hartnoll, Phyllis. The Oxford Companion to the Theatre. 4th Edition. New York: Oxford University Press, 1983.
Contains a biographical entry on Tandy.

B35 Hawkins, Jack. Anything for a Quiet Life. London: Hamish Hamilton, 1973.
Hawkins describes his "star-crossed" marriage to Tandy and his devotion to their daughter Susan.

B36 Hayman, Ronald. John Gielgud. New York: Random House, 1971.
Extensive account of Gielgud's 1934 Hamlet on the West End with Tandy as Ophelia and the popular 1932 West End success, Musical Chairs, again with Tandy in the cast.

B37 Henderson, Mary C. Theater in America: 200 Years of Plays, Players, and Productions. New York: Harry N. Abrams, Inc., Publishers, 1986.
Contains two photos of Tandy in Streetcar. The author wrote that British-born Jessica Tandy shed her English accent and played with unfailing skill and sensitivity.

B38 Herbert, Jan. Who's Who in the Theatre. 17th Edition. Detroit, MI: Gale Research, 1981.
Includes a biographical sketch of Tandy.

B39 Holden, Anthony. Laurence Olivier. New York: Atheneum, 1988.
Tandy was interviewed for this biography and is quoted on various Olivier performances, including the television filming of The Moon and Sixpence.

B40 International Motion Picture Almanac 1984. 55th Edition. New York: Quigly Publishing, 1984.
Contains a list of Tandy's films made between 1955 and 1982, including brief biographical data.

B41 Ireland, Normal Olin. Index to Women of the World from Ancient to Modern Times: Biographies and Portraits. Westwood, MA: F. W. Faxon Company, 1970.
Contains several biographical sources on Tandy.

B42 Jones, David Richard. Great Directors At Work: Stanislavsky, Brecht, Kazan, Brook. Berkeley: University of California Press, 1986.
The Streetcar success story is retold with the suggestion that Tandy thought her special performance in Portrait of a Madonna "absolutely disastrous" and that producer Irene Selznick

resisted the casting of Tandy as Blanche DuBois because the actress had not been either a huge success in films or had worked in the New York theatre for five years.

**B43** Kazan, Elia. Elia Kazan: A Life. New York: Alfred A. Knopf, 1988.
Kazan describes rehearsals for the stage production of A Streetcar Named Desire and the contrasting working styles of Jessica Tandy and Marlon Brando.

**B44** Kerr, Walter. Journey to the Center of the Theater. New York: Alfred A. Knopf, 1979.
Contains a review of Tandy as Lady Wishfort in 1976 Stratford Festival (Canada) production of The Way of the World.

**B45** Leiter, Samuel L. The Encyclopedia of the New York Stage 1920-1930. 2 Vols. Westport, CT: Greenwood Press, 1985.
An entry on The Matriarch (1930) with Constance Collier and the twenty year-old Tandy.

**B46** Leiter, Samuel L. Ten Seasons: New York Theatre in the Seventies. Westport, CT: Greenwood Press, 1986.
Comparison of Tandy and Cronyn to the Lunts.

**B47** Leiter, Samuel L. Shakespeare Around the Globe: A Guide to Notable Postwar Revivals. Westport, CT: Greenwood Press, 1986.
Entries include A Midsummer Night's Dream at the Stratford Festival Theatre with Tandy as Hippolyta/Titania and Macbeth and Troilus and Cressida at the American Shakespeare Festival with Tandy as Lady Macbeth and Cassandra.

**B48** Little, Stuart W. Off-Broadway: The Prophetic Theater. New York: Coward, McCann & Geoghegan, Inc. 1972.
Brief discussions of Tandy's involvement in the first seasons of the Phoenix Theatre, New York, and the Guthrie Theater, Minneapolis.

**B49** Little, Stuart W. and Arthur Cantor. The Playmakers. New York: W. W. Norton & Company, 1970.
Discussion of mutual competitiveness that pervades acting families, including the Cronyns.

**B50** The London Stage 1920-1929: A Calendar of Plays and Players. 3 vols. Ed. J. P. Wearing. Metuchen, NJ: The Scarecrow Press, Inc., 1984.
Contains four entries on Tandy.

**B51** May, Robin. A Companion to the Theatre: The Anglo-American Stage from 1920. London: Lutterworth, 1973.
Contains information on productions.

**B52** Miller, Jordan Y. Twentieth Century Interpretations of "A Streetcar Named Desire." Englewood Cliffs, NJ: Prentice Hall, 1971.
Contains first-night responses by major critics to Tandy's performance as Blanche DuBois.

**B53** Nash, Jay Robert and Stanley Ralph Ross. Motion Picture Guide, 1927-1983. Chicago: Cinebooks Inc., 1985
Includes listing of Tandy's films.

**B54** Newquist, Roy. Showcase. New York: Morrow, 1966.
Contains an entry on Tandy.

**B55** Nightingale, Benedict. Fifth Row Center: A Critic's Year On and Off Broadway. New York Times Books, 1986.
The British critic for the New York Times describes the Broadway revival of The Glass Menagerie, directed by John Dexter, with Tandy as Amanda Wingfield. This critic found Tandy's performance "flat," "dogged," and "unpretentious."

**B56** Notable Names in the American Theatre. Clifton, NJ: James T. White and Co., 1976.
Contains a biographical entry on Tandy.

**B57** On Broadway. Photographs by Fred Fehl. Text by William Stott with Jane Stott. Austin: University of Texas Press, 1978.
Anecdotes about Tandy's Broadway plays along with Fehl's photographs of Tandy.

**B58** Palmer, Scott. British Film Actors' Credits 1895-1987. Jefferson, NC: McFarland, 1988.
Includes listing on Tandy.

**B59** Parish, James Robert. Actors' Television Credits 1950-1972. Metuchen, NJ: The Scarecrow Press, 1973.
Contains listing on Tandy's television credits.

**B60** Parker, John. The Dramatic List: Who's Who in the Theatre: A Biographical Record of the Contemporary Stage. 7th-12th Editions. London: Pitman, 1933-1957.
Includes biographical entry on Tandy.

**B61** Pettigrew, John and Jamie Portman. Stratford: The First Thirty Years. 2 Vols. Toronto: Macmillan, 1985.
Contains entries on Tandy's performances with the Stratford Festival Theatre.

**B62** Rehramer, George. The Macmillan Film Bibliography. New York: Macmillan, 1982.
Contains list of Tandy's films.

**B63** Rossi, Alfred. Astonish Us in the Morning: Tyrone Guthrie Remembered. London: Hutchinson Publishers, 1977.
A book of conversations with Tyrone Guthrie's friends and colleagues. In the section with Cronyn and Tandy, she describes Guthrie's staging of the opening scene of Hamlet and the scene of Lopahin's return in The Cherry Orchard.

**B64** Rossi, Alfred. Minneapolis Rehearsals: Tyrone Guthrie Directs Hamlet. Berkeley: University of California Press, 1970.
A record by his assistant director of Tyrone Guthrie's 1963 rehearsals for Hamlet. Contains quotes from a September 9, 1963 interview with Jessica Tandy who played Gertrude.

**B65** Schneider, Alan. Entrances: An American Director's Journey. New York: Viking Penguin, Inc., 1986.
Schneider describes his staging of Edward Albee's A Delicate Balance on Broadway with Tandy and Cronyn. He praised Tandy's portrayal of Agnes as "instinctive" and her voice and gestures "like music."

**B66** Screen World. Ed. John Willis. New York: Crown Publishers, Inc., 1966-.
Contains information and photographs on Tandy's films since 1966.

**B67** Selznick, Irene Mayer. A Private View. New York: Alfred A. Knopf, 1983.
Selznick tells the producer's version of the Streetcar story from Audrey Wood's call about a new play through the London production with Vivien Leigh. She wrote that Tandy's performance was so superb in Portrait of a Madonna that "we practically handed her Blanche there and then" (302).

**B68** Spoto, Donald. The Kindness of Strangers: The Life of Tennessee Williams. Boston: Little, Brown & Company, 1985.
Spoto records events surrounding the Los Angeles production of Portrait of a Madonna with

Tandy and the "special" performance for Selznick, Kazan, and Williams. He also describes the rehearsals and opening of A Streetcar Named Desire in 1947.

**B69** Sprigge, Elizabeth. Sybil Thorndike Casson. London: Victor Gollancz Ltd., 1971.
Brief mention of the productions of Yes, My Darling Daughter and Time and the Conways. Thorndike is cited as praising Tandy's performance in the latter.

**B70** Stevenson, Isabelle. The Tony Award. New York: Crown Publishers, 1987.
Includes list of nominations and wins for Tandy.

**B71** Terrace, Vincent. Encyclopedia of TV Series, Pilots, and Specials, 1973-1984. 3 Vols. New York: New York Zoetrope, 1985.
Includes entries on Tandy.

**B72** Terrace, Vincent. The Complete Encyclopedia of Television Programs 1947-1979. 2nd Edition. 2 Vols. New York: A. S. Barnes & Company, 1979.
Includes entries on Tandy.

**B73** Theatre World Annual (London) 1964: A Full Pictorial Review of the 1962-63 London Season. London: Iliffe Books Ltd., 1963.
Includes entry on production of Big Fish, Little Fish with Tandy and Cronyn.

**B74** Thomson, David. The Biographical Dictionary of Film. 2nd Edition. New York: William Morrow & Company, 1981.
Includes entries on Tandy's films.

**B75** Trewin, J. C. The Birmingham Repertory Theater 1913-1963. London: Barrie and Rockliff, 1963.
Contains list of plays produced by the company, including Tandy's professional debut in A Comedy of Good and Evil in 1928.

**B76** Trewin, J. C. The Theater since 1900. London: Andrew Dakers, Ltd., 1951.
Contains information on Tandy's early career.

**B77** Variety International Show Business Reference 1983. Ed. Mike Kaplan. New York: Garland Publishing Inc., 1983.
Tandy is listed in the Broadway Play credits.

**B78** *Variety Who's Who in Show Business*. Ed. Mike Kaplan. Revised Edition. New York: R. R. Bowker, 1989.
Contains entry on Tandy.

**B79** Vinson, John. *International Directory of Films and Filmmakers, Vol. III, Actors and Actresses*. Chicago: St. James Press, 1986.
Includes biographical data on Tandy.

**B80** Walker, Alexander. *Vivien: The Life of Vivien Leigh*. New York: Weidenfeld & Nicholson, 1987.
Discussion of Vivien Leigh's successful campaign for the screen role of Blanche DuBois, though, according to Walker, director Elia Kazan favored his own stage Blanche--Jessica Tandy.

**B81** Wearing, J. P. *American and British Theatrical Biography: A Directory*. Metuchen, NJ: Scarecrow Press Inc., 1979.
Contains six biographical sources on Tandy.

**B82** Webster, Margaret. *The Same Only Different: Five Generations of a Great Theatre Family*. New York: Alfred A. Knopf, 1969.
Discussion of the West End success of *Musical Chairs* in 1932 with John Gielgud, Margaret Webster, and Jessica Tandy in the cast.

**B83** *Who's Who in the Theatre: A Biographical Record of the Contemporary Stage*. Ed. Ian Herbert. 17th Edition. Detroit, MI: Gale Research Company, 1981.
Contains a biographical entry on Tandy.

**B84** *Who's Who of American Women (1970)*. 6th Edition. Chicago: Marquis Who's Who, Inc., 1971.
Includes a biographical entry on Tandy.

**B85** *A Who's Who of British Film Actors*. Ed. Scott Palmer. Metuchen, NJ: The Scarecrow Press, 1981.
Tandy is listed as a "character" actress of stage and film. Her films between 1932 and 1981 are also listed.

**B86** Williams, Dakin and Shepherd Mead. *Tennessee Williams: An Intimate Biography*. New York: Arbor House, 1983.
Discussion of the *Portrait of a Madonna* production with "a little-known actress," Jessica Tandy, who then was cast as Blanche DuBois. The book has an account of the opening-night of *A Streetcar Named Desire* and of Cronyn

and Tandy's brief interest in 1967 in performing in Williams' Two-Character Play.

**B87** Williams, Edwina Dakin. Remember Me To Tom. New York: G. P. Putnam's Sons, 1963.
This account of the "Streetcar story" by Tennessee Williams' mother contains only brief mention of Jessica Tandy. It largely concerns Irene M. Selznick as "another woman important in Tom's life."

**B88** Williams, Harcourt. Old Vic Saga. London: Winchester Publications Ltd., 1949.
Includes accounts of Tandy's work with the Old Vic in productions of Hamlet, King Lear, and The Tempest.

**B89** Williams, Tennessee. Memoirs. Garden City, NY: Doubleday & Company, 1975.
The playwright remembers that after seeing Jessica Tandy in Los Angeles in Portrait of a Madonna it was instantly apparent to him that "Jessica was Blanche."

**B90** Willis, John. Theatre World. New York: Crown Publishers, 1966-82.
Contains information and photographs on Tandy's Broadway and Off-Broadway performances.

**B91** Wood, Audrey with Max Wilk. Represented by Audrey Wood. Garden City, NY: Doubleday, 1981.
Tennessee Williams' long-time literary agent discusses the casting of A Streetcar Named Desire, tryout events, and the Broadway run. Wood records that during the Boston tryout Kazan turned to Williams and whispered, "This smells like a hit."

## INTERVIEWS, ARTICLES, FEATURES

**R01** Anne of England theatre review. The New York Times. October 8, 1945.

**R02** The Ante-Room theatre review. The Times (London). August 15, 1936.

**R03** Anthony and Anna. The Times (London). November 9, 1935. The New York Times. December 8, 1935.

**R04** Atkinson, Brooks. "First Night at the Theatre." The New York Times. December 4, 1947.

**R05** Atkinson, Brooks. "Phoenix Rises." The New York Times. December 20, 1953.

**R06** Atkinson, Brooks. "Streetcar Passenger." The New York Times. June 12, 1949.

**R07** Atkinson, Brooks. " 'Streetcar' Tragedy--Mr. Williams's Report on Life in New Orleans." The New York Times. December 14, 1947.

**R08** Autumn Crocus theatre review. The Times (London). April 7, 1931.

**R09** Barnes, Howard. "O'Neill Status Won by Author of 'Streetcar.'" The New York Herald Tribune. December 14, 1947.

**R10** Barranger, Milly S. "Three Women Called Blanche: Jessica Tandy, Uta Hagen, Vivien Leigh." Tennessee Williams Literary Journal (Spring 1989): 15-30.

**R11** Bedtime Story theatre review. The New York Times. April 16, 1959.

**R12** Below the Surface theatre review. The Times (London). January 11, 1932.

**R13** Brown, John Mason. "Southern Discomfort." The Saturday Review (December 27, 1947): 24.

**R14** Bulnes, J. "Les immortels du cinema: Jessica Tandy." Cine-Tele-Revue. December 15, 1988.

**R15** "Cards: Interview." New Yorker (October 24, 1977): 36-37.

**R16** Chambers, A. "Jessica Tandy and Hume Cronyn are Center Stage in the American Theater." People Weekly (June 2, 1986): 116-17.

R17 Chapman, John. "A Streetcar Named Desire" Sets Season's High in Acting, Writing." The New York Daily News. December 4, 1947.

R18 Chase, Chris. "Jessica Tandy Shuttles from Stage to Screen." The New York Times. April 10, 1981.

R19 Chase, Chris. "Tandy and Cronyn are Wed to the Theatre, Too." The New York Times. March 24, 1974.

R20 Children in Uniform theatre review. The New York Times. November 6, 1932.

R21 Clarke, G. "Two Lives, One Ambition." Time (April 2, 1990): 62-64.

R22 Darnton, N. "She Oughta Be in Pictures." Newsweek (January 1, 1990): 56-57.

R23 "Dartmouth Lists Drama Advisers." The New York Times. April 3, 1960.

R24 Diesel, Leota. "Round-the-Clock with the Cronyns." Theatre Arts. February 1952.

R25 Flatley, Guy. "Edward Albee Fights Back." The New York Times. April 18, 1971.

R26 Forsberg, Myra. "'Daisy' Blossoms Once More in Atlanta." The New York Times. June 4, 1989.

R27 Freedman, Samuel G. "Interview." The New York Times. November 27, 1983.

R28 Funke, Lewis. "32 Actors Form Theater Organization." The New York Times. June 15, 1971.

R29 Geneva theatre review. The New York Times. January 31, 1940.

R30 Gent, George. "New Beckett Play, 'Not I,' to Bow Here." The New York Times. August 29, 1972.

R31 Gibbs, Wolcott. "Lower Depths, Southern Style." New Yorker (December 13, 1947): 55.

R32 Glorious Morning theatre review. The Times (London). November 28, 1938. The New York Times. June 12, 1938.

R33 Gussow, Mel. "Cronyns Play 'Keys' as Ever--in Tune." The New York Times. March 1, 1974.

**R34** Hamlet theatre review. The Times (London). November 15, 1934. The New York Times. December 2, 1934.

**R35** Hayes, R. "Three for Two." Commonweal (May 22, 1959): 206.

**R36** Honour Thy Father theatre review. The Times (London). December 7, 1936.

**R37** Hughes, Charlotte. "Regarding Jessica Tandy." The New York Times. May 17, 1942.

**R38** Hughes, Elinor. "A Streetcar Named Desire." The Boston Herald. November 4, 1947.

**R39** Juarez and Maximilian theatre review. The Times (London). February 9, 1932.

**R40** Jupiter Laughs theatre review. The New York Times. September 10, 1940.

**R41** Kernan, Michael. "Jessica Tandy, Between the Lines." The Washington Post. December 23, 1982.

**R42** Kerr, Walter. "Beckett, Yes, But Also A Tandy-Cronyn Festival." The New York Times. December 3, 1972.

**R43** King Lear theatre review. The New York Times. April 28, 1940.

**R44** Kleiman, Dena. "For Tandy and Cronyn, a New Play Echoes Years of Partnership." The New York Times. April 20, 1986.

**R45** Knelman, M. "First Family." Macleans 91 (February 6, 1978): 38-40.

**R46** Kroll, Jack. "Theatre: Old Cards." Newsweek (October 17, 1977): 117.

**R47** Krutch, Joseph Wood. "Drama." The Nation (December 20, 1947): 686.

**R48** Lady Audley's Secret theatre review. The Times (London). January 23, 1933.

**R49** Laskas, J. M. "Happily Ever After." Life (April 1990): 76-78.

**R50** The Last Enemy theatre review. The New York Times. October 31, 1930.

**R51** Line Engaged theatre review. The Times (London). October 25, 1934.

**R52** The Man Who Pays the Piper theatre review. The Times (London). February 11, 1931.

**R53** Matonsek, M. Harper's Bazaar (January 1990): 58.

**R54** The Matriarch theatre review. The New York Times. March 19, 1930.

**R55** Midsummer Fires theatre review. The Times (London). May 22, 1933.

**R56** Musical Chairs theatre review. The New York Times. November 16, 1931.

**R57** Mutual Benefit theatre review. The Times (London). July 11, 1932.

**R58** Nathan, George Jean. "The Streetcar Isn't Drawn by Pegasus." The New York Journal-American. December 15, 1947.

**R59** Now I Lay Me Down to Sleep theatre review. The New York Times. July 23, 1949.

**R60** Norton, Elliot. "Plot But No Pity in A Streetcar Named Desire." Boston Post. November 9, 1947.

**R61** Norton, Elliot. "Tennessee Williams Play Opens." Boston Post. November 4, 1947.

**R62** Playbill. November 1983.

**R63** Popkin, Henry. "In Canada--From Classics To Tryouts." The New York Times. September 7, 1980.

**R64** Portrait of a Madonna theatre review. The New York Times. April 16, 1959.

**R65** Port Said theatre review. The Times (London). November 2, 1931.

**R66** Porter, A. "Tandy arrives on a Streetcar." Collier's. April 17, 1948.

**R67** A Pound on Demand theatre review. The New York Times. April 26, 1959.

**R68** Ormsbee, Helen. "The Girl on That New Orleans Streetcar." New York Herald Tribune. December 7, 1947.

**R69** Reif, Robin. Dial. March 1984.

**R70** Shaw, Irwin. "Theater: Masterpiece." New Republic (December 22, 1947): 34-35.

**R71** Seidenberg, R. "Driving Miss Daisy." American Film (January 1990): 59.

**R72** Simon, John and Rhoda Koenig. "Theatre: Jessica Tandy." New York (September 19, 1983): 52-53.

**R73** Stewart, R. S. "John Gielgud and Edward Albee Talk about the Theater." Atlantic Monthly (April 1965): 61-68.

**R74** Sullivan, Dan. "The Actor's Art: Jessica Tandy." Los Angeles Times "Calendar." March 25, 1984.

**R75** Tandy, Jessica. "One Year of Blanche Du Bois." The New York Times. November 28, 1948.

**R76** Ten-Minute Alibi theatre review. The Times (London). January 3, 1933; February 9, 1933.

**R77** "Theatre Arts Gallery." Theatre Arts (December 2, 1959): 30-32.

**R78** The Theatre of Life theatre review. The Times (London). April 6, 1929.

**R79** Time and the Conways theatre review. The New York Times. January 4, 1938.

**R80** Triple Play theatre review. The New York Times. April 26, 1959.

**R81** Tynan, Kenneth. "A for Effort, O for Obstinacy." New Yorker (April 25, 1959): 82.

**R82** Water theatre review. The Times (London). June 26, 1929.

**R83** Watts, Richard, Jr. "Streetcar Named Desire Is Striking Drama." The New York Post. December 4, 1947.

**R84** The White Steed theatre review. The New York Times. January 11, 1939.

**R85** White, Timothy. "Theater's First Couple." New York Times Magazine. December 26, 1982.

**R86** **Special Collections**

Memorabilia, papers, and photographs from the personal collections of Jessica Tandy and Hume Cronyn are deposited in the Manuscript Division of The Library of Congress, Washington, D. C.

The Performing Arts Research Center of The New York Public Library at Lincoln Center, New York City, contains clippings, photographs, books and reviews related to Jessica Tandy's long career in the American theatre.

The Fred Fehl Collection (of photographs) is housed in the Hoblitzelle Theatre Arts Library in the Humanities Research Center of the University of Texas at Austin. In the collection are photographs of Jessica Tandy (and Hume Cronyn) in _Anne of England_, _The Fourposter_, _Madam, Will You Walk_, _The Man in the Dog Suit_, _Triple Play_, _Five Finger Exercise_, and others.

# Subject Index

The Subject Index lists alphabetically the career achievements, theatres, plays, films, television appearances, awards, recordings, individuals, and events important to the life and career of Jessica Tandy. This index makes use of both page numbers and section entry numbers (for example, **F01**, **S01**, **T01**, **D01**), for easy reference.


Academy of Motion Pictures and Sciences ("Oscar") Award, 11-12, 19, 28, 70, A06
Academy of Science Fiction, Fantasy, and Horror Films Awards, 27, A09
Act Without Words I, 24, S87
Actors Theatre of Louisville (KY), 51
Actors' Laboratory Theatre (Los Angeles), 18, S48
Adler, Luther, F10
Adventures of a Young Man, 21, F12
Ahmanson Theatre (Los Angeles), 26, S101
Albee, Edward, 1, 8, 9, 22, 23, S56, S58, S81
Aldredge, Theoni V., S56
Aldredge, Tom, F21
Aldwych Theatre (London), 6
Alexander, John, S50
Alice Sit-by-the-Fire, 2, 13, S02
Alley Theatre Award, 27, A09
All Over, 9, 23, S58
Ameche, Don, F20, F22
American Academy of Dramatic Arts Franklin Haven Sargent Award, 27, A09
American Shakespeare Festival Theatre (Stratford, CT), 7, 21, S72, S73
Anderson, Lindsay, S57
Anderson, Maxwell, F09
Anne of England, 18, S46
ANTA Theatre (New York City), 20, S69
The Ante-Room, 16, S31

Anthony and Anna, 16, S30
Anthony, C. L., 14, S12
Antoinette Perry ("Tony") Award, 6, 19, 25, 26, A01, A02, A03, A04, A05, B70
Armstrong, Anthony, 15, S20
Arsenic and Old Lace, S52
Arts Theatre (London), 14, 16, S05, S14, S21, S33
Atkinson, Brooks, 1, 5, 8, S41, S49, S50, S51, S54, B01 B02
Autumn Crocus, 2, 14, S12
Aykroyd, Dan, F24

Ballard, Lucinda, S49, S51
Barnes, Clive, S57, S58, S87, S88
Barr, Richard, S56, S58, S59
Barrie, James M., 13, S02
Barrymore, Lionel, F04
Bates, Alan, 11, 24, F14, D01
Batteries not Included, 11, 27, F21
Baxter, Anne, 24, S59
Bay, Howard, S50
Beckett, Samuel, 1, 8, 23, 24, S57, S87, S88
Bedford, Brian, S54
Bedtime Story, 21, S70
Belch, Albert, 21, S53
Below the Surface, 14, S15
Ben Greet Academy of Acting (London), 2, 13
Benton, Robert, F16
Beresford, Bruce, 11, F24
Best Friends, 11, 26, F17
The Better Half, T15
Beymer, Richard, 21, F12
Big Fish, Little Fish, 8, 21, S74
Biltmore Theatre (New York City), 18, S45
The Birds, 11, 22, F13
Birmingham Repertory Company (England), 2, 13, S02, B75
Birthday, 16, S25
Blyth, Ann, 19, F08
Borden, Ethel, S46
The Bostonians, 11, 26, F19
Boyer, Charles, 19, F08
Brandeis University, 12, 119
Brando, Marlon, 5, 6, S49
Brecht, Bertolt, 22, S80
Bridges, Beau, F15
Brimley, Wilford, F20, F23
Broadway, 1, 2, 3, 5, 6, 7, 8, 9, 10, 14, 19, 27, S08. S10, S37, S42, S45, S46, S47, S49, S50, S51, S52, S53, S54, S55, S56, S57, S58, S59, S60, S61, S62, S63, S64, B01
Brook, Peter, S55
Burton, Richard, D03
Bury, John, S55, S64
Butley, 11, 24, F14, D01

Caldwell, Zoe, S76, S78, S80
Cambridge Festival Theatre (England), 2, 15, S17

Camino Real, 8, 23, S85
Campbell, Douglas, S77, S78
The Canary Sedan, T15
Canby, Vincent, 107
Canfield, Mary Cass, 18, S46
Carradine, Keith, S62
Carroll, Leo G., 18, S46, F07, F10
Carroll, Paul Vincent, 3, 17, S39
The Caucasian Chalk Circle, 7, 22, S80
Celestin, Jack, 16, S27
Charles the King, 17, S41
Chekhov, Anton, 22, S76, S79, D02
The Cherry Orchard, 7, 22, S79, D02
Children in Uniform, 3, 15, S19
Christmas 'Til Closing, T05
City Center (New York City), 7, 20, S68
Clark, Brian, 7, 11, 26, S64
Cliff, Montgomery, D05
Close, Glenn, 26, F18
Clothes Make the Man, T15
Coburn, Charles, 18, F05
Coburn, D. L., 25, S60, T12
Cocoon, 11, 26, 101, 105, F20
Cocoon: The Return, 27, F23
Cohan, George M., 7
Cohen, Alexander H., S57
Collier, Constance, 2, 14, S08
Come into the Garden, Maude, 9, 24, S59
The Comedy of Good and Evil, 2, 13, S02
Commoedia Matinee Club Award, 7, A09
Common Wealth Award, 26, A09
Compton, Fay, S43
The Confidence Man, T15
Congreve, William, 22, S78, S91
Cooper, Gladys, F04, F05
Cooper, Susan, 25, S62, S97
Corey, Wendell, F11
Coriolanus, D03
Coronet Theatre (New York City), 19, 21, S50, S53
Corsaro, Frank, S52
Cort Theatre (New York City), 17, 25, S61
Cotton, Joseph, 19, F09
Coward, Noel, S59
Crawford, Cheryl, S52
Crisp, Donald, F04
Criterion Theatre (London), 16, S32
Cronin, A. J., 3, 18, S45, F05
Cronyn, Christopher Hume, 4, 18
Cronyn, Hume, 4, 5, 6, 7, 8, 9, 10, 11, 12, 18, 19, 20, 21, 22, 23, 24, 25, 26, 27, 28, 70, S48, S49, S50, S51, S52, S53, S56, S59, S60, S62, S64, S65, S66, S67, S68, S69, S70, S74, S76, S77, S79, S82, S87, S89, S95, S96, S97, S99, S101, F03, F05, F15, F18, F20, F21, F23, T03, T07, T12, T13, D02, D08, D09, A09
Cronyn, Tandy, 4, 7, 18, 28, T14
Crowther, Bosley, 81

Dahl, Roald, 20, S52
Daniels, Jeff, F22
Darnelle, Linda, 19, F07
Dartmouth College, 21
Davenport, Marcia, F04
Davies, Andrew, 25, S61
A Day by the Sea, 20, S69
de Hartog, Jan, 16, 20, S51, T06
De Leon, Jack, 16, S27
A Delicate Balance, 9, 22, 23, S56, S81, A09
Death of a Salesman, 7, 22, S77
Delia Austrian Medal, 8, A01, A09
Dennehy, Brian, F20
The Desert Fox, 4, 20, F10
Deutsch, Helen, F03
Devane, William, F15
Devine, George, 18, S28, S44
Dewhurst, Colleen, 23, 111, S58
Dexter, John, 11, 26, S63
Disney, Walt, F11
Drama Critics Circle Award (Los Angeles), A02
Drama Desk Award, 8, A02, A04, A07
Drama League Award, A01
Dragonwyck, 4, 18, F06
Driving Miss Daisy, 11, 27, 28, F24, A06
Duchess Theatre (London), 15, 17, S19, S38
Duerrenmatt, Friedrich, 8, 22, S55
Duke of York's Theatre (London), 8, 16, 21, S27, S74
Du Maurier, Daphne, F13

Eder, Richard, S60
Edwards, Ben, S52
Embassy Theatre (London), 15, S22
Emmy Award (television), 27, A08
The End of Blackbeard the Pirate, T15
Ervine, St. John, 16, S30
Ethel Barrymore Theatre (New York City), 1, 5, 7, 9, 19, 20, 24, 26, S49, S51, S59, S62
Eugene O'Neill Theatre (New York City), 26, S63
Evans, Maurice, 2, 14, S04
Eve, 8, 24, S93

Face to Face, 20
The Fallen Idol, T08
Ferrer, Jose, S51
Fineberg, Larry, 8, S93
Fisher, Jules, S57
Fitzgerald, Barry, 17, S39
The Five Dollar Bill, T15
Five Finger Exercise, 21, S54, S71, A09
Fontaine, Joan, 19, F09
Fontanne, Lynn, 7
Fordham University, 12, 26
Forever Amber, 4, 19, F07
Forum Theatre (New York City), 24, S87, S88
The Fourposter, 6, 7, 8, 24, S51, S67, S68, T06, A09

Foxfire, 7, 11, 25, 26, 27, S62, S97, S99, S101, T13, A04, A08
Freeman, Morgan, 11, 27, F24
French Without Tears, 16, S32

Garson, Greer, 18, F04
Geneva, 3, 17, S41, S42
Gielgud, John, 3, 8, 9, 14, 16, 17, 21, 23, S14, S28, S29, S43, S44, S54, S57, S58, B27, B28, B36
Gilford, Jack, F20, F23
The Gin Game, 7, 9-10, 25, S60, S95, S96, T12, A02
The Glass Eye, T15
Glass Flowers Never Drop Petals, T15
The Glass Menagerie, 11, 26, S49, S63, D04
Glorious Morning, 3, 17, S38
Glory in the Flower, T15
Gone With the Wind, 6
Coring, Marius, 18, S44
Grahame, Kenneth, D08, D09
Granville-Barker, Harley, 3, 17, S43
Gray, Simon, F14, D01
The Great Adventure, T15
The Green Years, 4, 18, F05
Grifasi, Joe, F15, F16
Grizzard, George, S75, S76
Guild Theatre (New York City), 18, S47
Guinness, Alec, 16, S28, S34, B30
Gussow, Mel, S59
The Guthrie Theater (Minneapolis), 7, 22, 25, S62, S75-77, S78-80, S99
Guthrie, Tyrone, 3, 7, 8, 16, 17, 22, 112, S34, S75, S76, S79, D02, B23, B31, B63, B64

Hall, Peter, S64
Hamilton, Diana, 16, S33
Hamlet, 3, 7, 16, 22, S28, S75
Hangman's House, T15
Happy Days, 7, 8, 24, S87, A07
Hardicke, Cedric, S69, F08, F10
Harris, Julie, D05
Harrison, Rex, 16, S32
Harvey, Frank, 14, S10
Hawkins, Jack, 2, 3, 15, 18, S13, S15, S28, B35
Hawkins, Susan Phyllida, 3, 4, 16
Hawn, Goldie, 26, F17
Haymarket Theatre (London), 15, S20
Hazlewood, C. H., 15, S21
Head, Edith, F13
"Hear America Speaking," 22
Heard, John, S63
Heartbreak House, 7, 23, S83, D05
Hedren, Tippi, 22, F13
Hemingway, Ernest, 109, F12
Henry V, 3, 16, 17, S35
Henry Miller's Theatre (New York City), 17, S42
Herbert, Jocelyn, S57

Hilda Crane, 6, 19, S50
Hill, George Roy, F18
Hingle, Pat, 21, S72, S73
Hitchcock, Alfred, 103, F13, T15
Hobson, Harold, 6
Hollywood, 4
Home, 9, 23, S57
The Honeys, 8, 20, S52
Honky Tonk Freeway, 11, 25, F15
Honour Thy Father, 16, S33
The House on Carroll Street, 27, F22
Howard, Sidney, 7, 20, S67
Howard, Trevor, 16, S32
Hughes, Barnard, F17
Hughes, Richard, 13, S02
Hunt, Hugh, S39
Hunt, J. L. F., 15, S15
Hunt, Linda, F19
Hunter, Kim, 5, 6, S49, S72, S73
Hunter, N. C., 20, S69
Hurt, Mary Beth, F18
Huston, Walter, F06, F09
Huxley, Aldous, F08

Icebound, T15
The Indiscretions of Eve, 2, 15, F01
The Inspector General, 2, 15, S17
Irving, John, F18
Ivory, James, F19

Jackson, Glenda, 25, S61
Jewison, Norman, F17
The John F. Kennedy Center Honors, 12, 27, A09
John Golden Theatre (New York City), 9, 25, 27, S64, S68
John Quincy Adams, T15
Johnson, Nunnally, F10
Jordan, Roy, 15, S18
Juarez and Maximilian, 15, S16
Jupiter Laughs, 3, 18, S45

Kazan, Elia, 5, 19, S49, B43
Kerr, Walter, S56
Kesselring, Joseph, 40
King Lear, 3, 17, S43
Knox, Alexander, S45
Komissarjevsky, Theodore, S14
Korda, Zoltan, F08
Kurtz, Swoosie, F18

Lady Audley's Secret, 3, 15, S21
Landau, Jack, S72, S73
Las Palmas Theatre (Los Angeles), 18
The Last Enemy, 2, 14, S10
Laughton, Charles, D07
Lee, Ming Cho, S63
Leigh, Vivien, 4, 6, 20, B21, B80

Leland Powers Honorary Award, 9, A09
Lewis, Cecil, 14, S07, F01
Light in the Forest, 11, 21, F11
Lincoln Center Repertory Company, S85
Line Engaged, 16, S27
Lithgow, John, F18
The Little Blue Light, 19, S66
Little Miss Bedford, T15
Longacre Theatre (New York City), 2, 14, 20, S08, S52, S63
Long Day's Journey into Night, 25, S94, S98
Long Distance, T09
Lunt, Alfred, 7
LuPone, Patti, F24
Lynley, Carol, 21, F11
Lyric Theatre (London), 25, S12, S96

MacArthur, James, 21, F11
Macbeth, 7, 21, S72
Mackenzie, Ronald, 14, S14
Macowan, Norman, 17, S38
Macready, George, F10
Madam, Will You Walk, 7, 20, S67
Madden, John, S100
Malden, Karl, 5, 6, S49
The Manderson Girls, 2, 13, S01
The Man in the Dog Suit, 8, 20, 21, S53
Mankiewicz, Joseph L., F06
The Man Who Pays the Piper, 14, S11
The Many Faces of Love, 24, T11
Marchand, Nancy, T19
Mark Taper Forum (Los Angeles), 7, 23, S82
The Marriage, T04
Marshall-Hole, Molly, 14, S06
Martin Beck Theatre (New York City), 8, 9, 22, 23, S53, S55, S58
Mason, James, 4, 20, F10
Mason, Marshall W., 25, S99
Masterpiece Playhouse, T02
Matalon, Vivian, S69
Mathews, Carmen, S53, S56
The Matriarch, 2, 14, S08
Maugham, W. Somerset, 49, T07
McCann, Elizabeth I., S61, S63
McDowall, Roddy, F02
McGillis, Kelly, 27, F22
The Merry Wives of Windsor, 16, S26
Metro-Goldwyn-Mayer (MGM), 3, B20
Midsummer Fires, 3, 15, S22
A Midsummer Night's Dream, 3, 8, 15, 24, S23, S92
Mielziner, Jo, S49
Miller, Arthur, 22, S77
Minnesota Theatre Company, 7, 22, S75-77, S78-80, D05
Moiseiwitsch, Tanya, S75, S76, S78, S79
The Miser, 7, 23, S82
Moliere, 7, 23, S82
The Moon and Sixpence, T07

Morosco Theatre (New York City), 9, 23, S57
Motley, S52, S72
Muni, Paul, S47
Munroe, C. K., 13, S04
Murder in the Family, 3, 17, F02
A Murder is Announced, T15
Murder Me Gently, T15
Musical Chairs, 14, S14
Music Box Theatre (New York City), 21, S54
Musser, Tharon, S54, S56, S72
Mutual Benefit, 3, 15, S18

National Medal of Arts Award, 12, 28, A09
National Press Club Award, A02
Natwick, Mildred, F08
Nelson, Ruth, S76, S78, S79, D02
Newman, Paul, 21, F12
New Theatre (London), 16, S28, S29
New York Drama Critics Circle Award, 6, S63
New York Shakespeare Festival Public Theatre, 26, S100
Nesbitt, Cathleen, 15, S19, S43
Nichols, Dandy, 9, S57
Nichols, Mike, 25, S60
Noah, 16, S29
Noel Coward in Two Keys, 9, 24, S59, S90
Not I, 23, 24, S88, S89, A07
Now I Lay Me Down to Sleep, 19, S65
Nugent, Nelle, S61, S63

Obey, Andre, 16, S29
O'Brien, Kate, 16, S31
O'Casey, Sean, 20, 21, S70
Oenslager, Donald, S53
Off-Broadway 7, 24, B48
Old Vic Company, 3, 8, 16, 17, 18, S35, S43, S44, B87
Olivier, Laurence, 3, 6, 16, 17, S34, S35, T07, B15, B39
Omnibus, T03
O'Neill, Eugene, 8, 25, S63, S98
Onstage: 25 Years at the Guthrie, T15
Open Air Theatre (London), 15, 17, S23, S40
Outer Circle Critics Award, A04
Oxford University Dramatic Society, 2, 14, S09

Page, Geraldine, F15
Page, Louise, 11, 26, S100
Parker, Fess, F11
Pastene, Robert, S75, S78, S79, D02
Patinkin, Mandy, F22
Paston, George, 14, S05
Peck, Gregory, 18, F03
The Petition, 7, 11, 27, A05, S64
Phillips, Robin, 8, 25, S91, S94
Phillpotts, Eden and Adelaide, 13, S03
Phoenix Theatre (New York City), 7, 20, S67
The Physicists, 8, 22, S55

Pinter, Harold, S57, F14, D01
Pleshette, Suzanne, F13
Plummer, Amanda, S63, F18
Portrait of a Madonna, 4-5, 18, 21, S48, S49, S70, T01
Port Said, 14, S13
Pound on Demand, 21, S70
Preminger, Otto, F07
Price, Vincent, 18, F06
Priestley, J. B., 3, 17, S37
Promenade All, 9, 23, S86
Pulitzer Prize, 6, 9, S49, S56, A01, A02
Punishments, Cruel and Unusual, T15

Quayle, Anthony, S28
Queen's Theatre (London), 16, S31

Raphaelson, Samson, 6, 19, S50
Rattigan, Terence, 16, S32
Redgrave, Vanessa, 11, 26, F19
Reed, Mark, 17, S36
Reeves, Christopher, 26, F19
Regional theatre, 7, 8
Repertory Theatre of Lincoln Center (New York City), 7-8, 23, S87, S88
Reynolds, Burt, 26, F17
Rich, Frank, 11, S61, S62, S63, S64
Richardson, Lee, 23, S57, S75, S76, S76, S79, D02
Richardson, Ralph, 9, 23, S45-46
Richter, Conrad, F11
Ritman, William, S56, S59
Ritt, Martin, F12
Ritz Theatre (New York City), 17, S37
Robson, Flora, 18, S21, S46
Robison, David E., 23, S86
Rolle, Esther, F24
The Romantic Young Lady, 16, S24
Rose, 25, S61, A03
Rose Without a Thorn, 2, 15, S17
Roth, Ann, F15, F18
Royal Court Theatre (London), 9, S57
The Rumour, 2, 13, S04
Ruta, Ken, S75, S77, S78, S79, D02
Ryan, Elaine, 19, S65

Sackler, Howard, D05
St. James Theatre (New York City), 18
St. James's Theatre (London), 17, S36, B19
St. Martin's Theatre (London), 14, S11, S18
Salonika, 11, 26, S100
Samuel Beckett Festival, 8, 23, 24
Saperstein, David, F20, F22
Sarah Siddons Award (Chicago), A02
Scheider, Roy, 26, F16
Schlesinger, John, F15
Schneider, Alan, 8, 9, 22, 23, 24, S56, S87, S88, B65
The School Mistress, T15

Schwary, Ronald I., F21
See Naples and Die, 2, 15, S17
Seghers, Anna, F03
Seldes, Marian, S56, F11
Selznick, Irene M., 4, 5, S49, B67
September Affair, 11, 19, F09
The Servant of Two Masters, 2-3, 15, S17
Seton, Anya, F06
The Set-up, T15
The Seventh Cross, 4, 18, F03
Shaffer, Peter, 21, S54
Shakespeare, William, 1, 2, 3, 7, 8, 20, S09, S17, S26,
    S28, S34, S35, S40, S43, S44, S72, S73, S75, S92, D03
The Shaw Festival (Niagara-on-the-Lake, Canada), 7, 23, S83
    D04
Shaw, George Bernard, 3, 17, 23, S40, S83
Shaw, Glen Byam, S28
Sherwood, Madeleine, S58
Shubert, Lee, 2, 14
Shubert Theatre (New York City), S10
Simpson, Lillian E., 2
Smith, Dodie, 14, S12
Smith, Maggie, S91
Smith, Oliver, S54
Solar Theater, Inc., 23
A Song at Twilight, 9, 24, S59
Stapleton, Maureen, 111, F20, F23
Stars Over Broadway, D06
Stern, G. B., 14, S08, S11
Stevens, Roger L., S64
Still of the Night, 11, 26, F16
Stoker, H. G., 15, S15
Storey, David, 9, 23, S57
The Story Lady, 28, T14
Stratford Shakespeare Festival Theatre (Ontario, Canada),
    8, 25, S62, S79, S91-93, S97-98, B61
Streep, Meryl, 26, F16
A Streetcar Named Desire, 1, 4, 5, 6, 8, 10, 12, 19, 37,
    56, 58, S49, D06, A01, B52
Stritch, Elaine, F23
Sudermann, Hermann, 15, S22

Tandy, Jessica
    awards, 25, 26, 27, 117-19
    birthplace, 1, 13
    Broadway appearances, 35-57
    children, 3, 4, 16, 18
    early years, 1-2, 13
    early film career, 2-3, 15, 65-66
    early stage career, 2-3, 13-17, 29-34
    education, 1-2, 13
    films, 65-107
    Hollywood years, 18-19, 67-77
    honorary degrees, 12, 24, 26, A10
    interviews with, 2, 3, 6, 9, 11, 12
    marriage to Cronyn, 4, 18

marriage to Hawkins, 3, 15
Off-Broadway appearances, 58-64
parents, 1
professional debut, 2, 13
recordings, 113-15
television, 109-112
Taubman, Howard, S55, S72, S73
Taylor, Rod, 22, F13
Tchin-Tchin, 23, S84
The Tempest, 3, 8, 17, S44
Ten-Minute Alibi, 15, S20
Tennessee Williams' South, T10
Theatre Guild on the Air, D07
Theatre Hall of Fame, 11, 25, A09
Theatre LA Annual Ovation Award, 28, A09
Theatre London (Ontario, Canada), 8, 24, 25, S94
Theatre of Life, 2, 14, S05
Thorndike, Sybil, 3, 17, S37, B69
The Three Sisters, 7, 22, S76
Tierney, Gene, 18, F06
Time and the Conways, 3, 17, S37
Tracy, Spencer, 4, 18, F03
Trainer, David, 26, S101
Triple Play, 8, 20, 21, S70
Tobias and the Angel, 17, S41
Toby, T15
Troilus and Cressida, 2, 7, 15, 21, S09, S17, S73
Twelfth Night, 2, 3, 14, 16, 17, S26, S34, S40
Twelfth Night Club Award, 6, A01
Twentieth Century-Fox, 4

Uhry, Alfred, 11-12, F24
The Unknown Warrior, 2, 14, S07
University of Western Ontario, 12, 24, 119, A10
U. S. Treasury, T15

The Valley of Decision, 4, 18, F04
Verdon, Gwen, F20, F23
Vernon, Frank, 14
The Village Voice Off-Broadway ("Obie") Award, 8, 24, A07
Vivian Beaumont Theatre (New York City), 23, S85
Voskovec, George, S55, S58
Vosper, Frank, S14, S28, F10

Waiting for Godot, 46
Wallis, Hal B., F09
War Against War, T15
Washbourne, Mona, 23, S57
Water, 2, 14, S06
The Way of the World, 7, 8, 22, 24, S78, S91
Webster, Margaret, 14, S14, B82
Weill, Kurt, F09
Werfel, Franz, 15, S16
West End, 2, 6
Wheeler, Hugh, 21
The White Steed, 3, 17, S39

Whitehead, Paxton, S83, D04
Whitehead, Robert, S55, S64
Who's Afraid of Virginia Woolf?, 45
Wickwire, Nancy, S78, D02
Wilde, Cornell, 19, F07
Wilder, Clinton, S56, S57
Williams, Emlyn, 14, 18, S13, S47
Williams, Robin, 26, F18
Williams, Tennessee, 1, 4, 5, 8, 11, 18, 20, 21, 23, 26, S48, S49, S63, S70, S85, D05, T01, T10, T11, B18, B68, B86, B89
Wilson, Edmund, 19, S66
The Wind in the Willows, D08, D09
Winsor, Kathleen, F07
The Witch, 2, 15, S17
A Woman's Vengeance, 4, 19, F08
Wood, Audrey, 5, B91
The World According to Garp, 11, 26, F18
Wright, William H., 21, S53
Wyndham's Theatre (London), 14, S13

Yates, Peter, F22
Yellow Sands, 2, 13, S03
Yes, My Darling Daughter, 17, S36
Yesterday's Magic, 18, S47
Young, Desmond, F10

Zanuck, Darryl F., F06
Zanuck, Richard D., F20, F23, F24
Zipprodt, Patricia, S63

## About the Author

MILLY S. BARRANGER is Professor and Chairperson of the Department of Dramatic Art at The University of North Carolina at Chapel Hill, and Executive Producer of PlayMakers Repertory Company. She is the author of several books and articles on theatre and drama, and is co-editor, with Alice M. Robinson and Vera Mowry Roberts, of *Notable Women in the American Theatre: A Biographical Dictionary* (Greenwood Press, 1989).